MAKING THEIR OWN PEACE

Twelve Women of Jerusalem

Ann N. Madsen (signature)

Ann N. Madsen

Christmas 2003

For Susan,
This should all seem
familiar — these amazing
women inspire me and
I hope you will find
inspiration in their
unique lives, too

n love,
Ann Madsen

Lantern Books • New York
A Division of Booklight Inc.

2003
Lantern Books
One Union Square West, Suite 201
New York, NY 10003

Printed in Canada

Text and photographs from *Our Jerusalem*, by Bertha Spafford Vester, are used with permission. Family photographs used by permission of the subjects and their families. All other photographs by Ann N. Madsen.

Library of Congress Cataloging-in-Publication Data

Madsen, Ann N. (Ann Nicholls)
  Making their own peace : twelve women of Jerusalem / Ann N. Madsen.
    p. cm.
  ISBN 1-59056-047-7 (alk. paper)
  1. Women—Jerusalem—Biography. 2. Palestinian women—Jerusalem—Biography. 3. Women and peace. 4. Jerusalem—Ethnic relations. 5. Arab-Israeli conflict—1993—Peace. I. Title.
  HQ1728.5.Z75A3 2003
  305.4'092'2569442—dc21

                    2003000404

printed on 100% post-consumer waste paper, chlorine-free

THIS IS A BOOK ABOUT PEACE. ITS SETTING IS JERUSALEM. It is about personal, not political, strategies. It is a primer for peace illustrated by the lives of twelve women who have searched for peace and have, in a measure, found it.

My venerable friend Ephraim Wagner wrote to me from Jerusalem in the aftermath of a just-failed summit, "I'm sick of building bridges that are never finished. We must each be a bridge!"

Within these pages are the firsthand accounts of women who understand what it means to become a bridge and have wittingly or unwittingly chosen to be one.

*To Truman, for taking me to Jerusalem,
and to the women I met there*

CONTENTS

Binyanei
Ha'Ooma

Mahane
Yehuda

Der Yassin

Hebrew
University
(Giv'at Ram)

Monastery of the Holy Cross
(Greek Orthodox)

0   1   2
km

Ramallah and
Shuafat

Hyatt Hotel

MOUNT SCOPUS

SHEIK JARRAH

Hebrew
University

Jerusalem Center for
Near Eastern Studies

American Colony Hotel

Augusta Victoria
Hospital

Dar El Tifl

MEA SHEARIM

MUSRARA
Herod's
Gate

Princess Basma
Center for Children

Damascus
Gate

Ancient
Sheep Market

Yehuda St

Moslem
Quarter

Makassed
Hospital

New Gate

OLD
CITY

Christian
Quarter

Bethany

Jaffa
Gate

Dome of
the Rock

MOUNT OF OLIVES

Agron St

Jewish
Quarter

Armenian
Quarter

Panorama
Hotel

BAKA

JERUSALEM

Bethlehem
(Church of the Nativity)

1. A Word about Jerusalem

Oh, how I love Jerusalem!

I love the way it looks, its bright white buildings reflecting a desert sunlight already overbright. I love the jumble and colors of the marketplaces, old and new. I love the women, who look as if they are in costume but aren't—they simply dress as did the women who, millennia before them, walked down these same cobbled streets.

I love the sunsets and sunrises. They sweep across the city, brushing its white stones with morning and evening gold. I love the quiet magic of the early mornings, when the dew, which has settled like a smoggy cloud over the city, disappears as the sun rises. And I always pause to catch the sunset before it is lost in the winding-down bustle of the day. Each afternoon's light is unique. One rosy gold dusk may be bright and cloudless, while the rainy season's deep magenta clouds are darkly ominous.

Often, both sunrise and sunset are accompanied by the call to prayer of many muezzin from their minarets.[1] Today their plaintive chant is electronically amplified. Happily, I heard them before modern technology was used to reach the faithful, who await their five-times-daily reminder to pray.

The prayer sounds of Jerusalem are strangely dear to me. Added to the sounds of the muezzin in their minarets are the myriad bells tolling from Christian churches. When a shofar is sounded on Jewish holy days, these three world religions come clanging together in one prayerful cacophony.[2]

I love the smells of the city. Walking through the Old City, one encounters a chaotic mixture of odors. Sweet mint is sold from the laps of Arab women in embroidered black dresses, who sit cross-legged on the ground at nearly every corner. In the Christian Quarter, myrrh and frankincense are displayed alongside the souvenirs. The spice shops with their bulging gunnysacks are a photographer's dream of color and texture. The pungent perfume of zatar and cumin and licorice-scented anise hangs heavy on the air.[3] Donkeys, camels and sheep share the way, so the strong smell of animal droppings is ever present, and everywhere tobacco smoke wafts upward and away. The crowded market streets are also pungent with the ever-present odor of the masses who pass through them daily.

I first encountered the sights, sounds and smells of this remarkable city in 1968. My husband and I had come to Jerusalem from Egypt, tracing the path the Holy Family had taken on their return two thousand years before. We arrived exhausted, late at night. I remember nothing but darkness and an overwhelming desire to sleep. I awakened in our small hotel on the southern end of the Mount of Olives at the sound of a rooster crowing.

I was disoriented at first. I remembered dimly that this was the Panorama Hotel—that I was truly in Jerusalem. It was so peaceful and quiet. Then the quiet was broken by a clanking sound that grew louder as it came closer. Curiosity dragged me from my comfortable bed. I pulled back the drapes.

I was awestruck. The sun was well up behind me, and I was bathed in brilliant light. Was it the effect of all the white stone buildings or the sun reflecting off the golden dome of the gigantic mosque?

From the tiny balcony, it seemed the Old City was right in my lap. It seemed so much larger than life. After gazing for a few moments, I became aware again of the now-intrusive clanking. A green and brown camouflaged tank rumbled down the hillside. At the time I had no idea how symbolic this sight would become.

That morning at the hotel breakfast buffet I met the Reverend Samuel Kemble. Tourists, especially those who think of themselves as pilgrims, often feel a certain ease visiting with other strangers and foreigners. The Reverend Kemble introduced himself, explaining that he was a minister from England—his speech had already disclosed that fact—and he wondered if he might hitch a ride on our bus to Masada that day. In that quizzical way Englishmen have of speaking, he asked me, "This is your first trip to Jerusalem, then?" I nodded and he looked at me knowingly. "It will not be your last. I, Nebi Samuel, prophesy."[4]

I pondered his words as we trudged up the Roman ramp on the west side of Masada that morning. The tourist experience was different in 1968. No tram was available to take us to the top of Masada, as there is today. And indeed, there were relatively few tourists in Jerusalem at that time—exactly one year after the Six Day War— though my sandals got dusty from trudging in and out of the most popular sites with a crowd of others.

One place we visited, which pilgrims had sought out for thousands of years, was the Sheep Market, located at a crossroads on the northeast corner of the Old City. There, sheep, goats, donkeys and camels were bartered or exchanged in an empty area walled in on three sides by ancient stone walls. It must have looked much the same for hundreds, maybe thousands, of years.

Then as in the past, men and boys came early in the morning, leading or carrying their animals. Animals, carts and cars always mix on the streets of Jerusalem. Even on the roads leading out of the city, our bus stopped more than once for a flock of sheep or goats to cross the street. But each Friday morning at that corner there was a traffic jam to end all traffic jams. Cars and buses waited for the bustle of this necessary commerce in animals. I noticed particularly a small lamb or kid being carried by a young boy.

Since 1968 Jerusalem has expanded beyond the now-deserted Sheep Market in the northeast corner of the Old City walls. Those walls, built by Suleiman, the Ottoman sultan, around A.D. 1520, cannot contain the city of today.

Teddy Kollek, longtime mayor of Jerusalem, was fond of comparing his growing city to the boroughs of New York, hoping that someday its diverse citizenry would adopt this dream. At age ninety-two, he continues to hold to his vision of One Jerusalem, made up of many peaceful parts. But in today's embattled city, geographical divisions often represent a deeper divide between the inhabitants who share this bitterly contested land.

Between Palestinian East Jerusalem and Israeli West Jerusalem is the city within a city called Mea Shearim, which means "one hundred gates." Those gates are, in effect, closed to as many influences of the world outside as possible. Ultra-orthodox Jews live in this closed society. Even their appearance speaks loudly of their belief.

Of course, this orthodox community represents only a small portion of Jerusalem's Jewish population, which is scattered throughout the city. And surrounding Jerusalem is a ring of settlements filled variously with orthodox, semi-religious, and insistently secular Jews. Their towns have become pieces in a political chess game of gigantic proportions. With the slogan "Land for Peace," the peace process snails along, sputters, halts, and resumes again. Meanwhile, the families in these settlements live on the ragged edge of uncertainty, though many claim nothing can move them from their homes.

In the Sinai, the handful of Jewish settlers who had built their homes and lives there were relocated when Israeli prime minister Menachem Begin exchanged that land with Egyptian president Anwar Sadat as part of a peace agreement between Egypt and Israel. President Sadat took home an uneasy peace, symbolized by his holding political title to the Sinai.

Egypt, the Sinai and Israel

The Jewish settlers in the Sinai then were only hundreds compared to the thousands who now occupy the settlements around Jerusalem, in the rest of the West Bank, and in the Golan Heights. Time and the extent of their hunger for peace will ultimately define borders and dictate who stays and who goes.

A small minority of Christians also resides in Jerusalem. The handful of Armenians, Greek Orthodox, Catholic, Lutheran, and other denominations maintain a low profile, content to live and work in the city where Christ walked and taught. Each claims its own real estate, its own venerated, holy space. Many of the sites overlap, however, and buildings jointly owned represent unresolved conflicts of interest. Each group maintains and defends its own traditions and history in this ancient city. But when the roof leaks in a jointly owned structure—such as the Church of the Holy Sepulchre in the center of the Old City or the Church of the Nativity in Bethlehem—the need for exclusive control sometimes overshadows the need for cooperation and tolerance.

Villages and cities nestle among the settlements. Here live many of the Palestinians (we used to say Arabs, but Palestinians better defines their nationalistic aspirations today). Once when I visited in one of those villages, my hostess invited me to drive my Subaru with its yellow Israeli license plates into her garage so she could shut the door and hide it.[5] That way her neighbors would not see that she had what seemed to be an Israeli visitor. These are the kinds of concerns that color daily life.

Many Palestinians also live in the Old City and in neighborhoods in greater Jerusalem. Some have lived in the country for centuries. For more than five decades, they have lived under an Israeli government. Recently, the uprising, or Intifada, that began in 2000 has focused world attention on their dream of a Palestinian state. Today, the Palestinians grapple with the daily, almost hourly, changes of a peace process begun secretly in Oslo, made public in Madrid, and frustrated at Camp David. Reticent handshakes on the White House lawn didn't move the process along, either. As Palestinians were slowly granted more and more land of their own, the problems inherent in self-governance emerged.

While agreement after agreement is violated by violence, both sides wait and watch as the peace process ebbs and flows, but mostly ebbs. Retaliation is a national policy of both the Palestinian Authority and the Israelis. Because of continuing retaliation, tragedy follows tragedy, like a snake giving birth to a snake (Isaiah 14:29).

It would be difficult to understand the women of Jerusalem without reference to the political threads that entangle their daily lives. Events in the region change attitudes and decisions frequently, often instantly. The rules of the game shift overnight. *Bitahone,* or "security," is a word peppering Israeli news. The thirst for news can be better understood when one realizes that if a war breaks out in this tiny country, it could be at one's own front door in minutes.

Once, tourist guides knew which cities to avoid: Ramallah, Nablus, Hebron and occasionally Bethlehem. But all that has changed. No city is safe. The tourist trade in Israel has shut down, which means hotels, restaurants, and merchants have shut down, too.

That is the context for the lives of the women whose stories follow. The Jerusalem economy is flat. Palestinians, Jews and Christians live with terror as their neighbor, never knowing when a bus, a street, a market, or their own village will explode around them. Yet they continue to hope for eventual peace. In the meantime, they make their own peace.

I look back to an evening on that first trip in 1968 when I walked alone up a narrow way that wound over the Mount of Olives. I felt completely safe, even after the sun had nearly disappeared. A young boy passed me, hurrying up the hill. He smiled, but we didn't speak. It made no difference whether he was Christian, Muslim or Jew. At that dusky moment, I pictured the boy Jesus walking the same road from Jerusalem to Bethany just over the mountain.

The next morning I met a Bedouin woman in a black dress with red cross-stitching on the bodice, her face partly hidden by a black veil. The embroidery seemed out of place to me, as if the woman had dressed up for some special occasion but had no place to go. Instead, she was covered with dust and dirt, going about her day's work.

In her tent-home on the edge of the desert, we communicated mostly with our hands and an occasional smile. I wondered about the unique conditions of birth that had dropped her into this thirsty wilderness and me into a fertile green valley five thousand miles away. Would she ever travel more than a few meters from her goat's-hair tent? I would climb back on a bus and drive away from the dust and heat; she would settle down once more to her baking of daily bread and tending the flock of dirty children racing around the corner of the tent, waiting to be fed.

As the days rushed by, I became more aware of the women of the region. The first line of a poem kept repeating itself in my mind: "God fashioned me for feeding and set me in a hungry land."[6] How did the women survive in this hungry land?

Little did I know then that this was only my first visit to Jerusalem and that I would return every year for over thirty years. More than I could imagine in those days has happened to me in this land. Once I stayed for nearly five years in my home just a mile north of the now-aging Panorama Hotel. Nebi Samuel was truly a prophet. But even he had not suggested I might become a resident, soaking up the city's long history and rich culture. I would no longer camp temporarily in hotels but would live in an apartment on the other side of the Mount of Olives. I would learn about the women of Jerusalem up close and over time as I explored and grew to love their city—and them.

As I met the women of Jerusalem—Muslims, Jews and Christians, including the easily recognizable nuns—the question welled up in me: "Why do they stay here through war after war?" I needed to know, and so I began to ask. The twelve women whose stories are told in this volume gave me my answer. They represent the thousands of women who live and work every day in the Eternal City. Their individual lives are amazing, marvelous in their persistence. Each had moments when she didn't know that a thing couldn't be done, so she just went ahead and did it. What made such courage possible?

I believe the answer lies in the vision of peace they kept in their hearts and maintained amidst the smoke of war or Intifada. It was as if they manufactured peace as they went along. It was homemade.

They kept hope alive when their efforts were frustrated by bureaucratic red tape or when the tedium of daily life grew oppressive. A vital
energy carried each one along, fueled by her faith or her sense of life's
meaning. I was inspired by their common determination not to count
the cost, never keeping emotional receipts for later reimbursement.
When tragedies burst into their lives, they chose not to spend their
energy on blame and anger, investing it instead in more important,
more promising projects. And they understood that in blaming others
we walk away from opportunities to solve our own problems.

I have gathered the stories of twelve women of Jerusalem as they
spoke for themselves, in their own words. I have tried to express their
truth, yet it is surely colored by my own. While I approached this
project with certain expectations, I found that my relationship with
each woman interviewed deepened my understanding and took me in
directions I had never imagined.

I offer you my vantage point, having observed their lives up close,
like a lens on a camera that gradually slides along until blurred features come into sharper focus and even faded colors brighten. These
women are clearly defined for me in living color.

They are women of courage. They are women with missions,
though they rarely speak in such terms. They believe themselves to
be ordinary, conceding only that they have accomplished extraordinary things. These women have remembered or rediscovered that
what may appear to be impossible can really be accomplished.

They have lived the impossible.

They are women who love deeply. Love is their common gift, and
they give it freely. From their abundant hearts they demonstrate with
their lives that there need be no scarcity of love in this world—that
even the orphan child can find love, and learn to be a loving parent
herself. It is not always easy, and they may sometimes give their portion haltingly, but they give all they have. Circumstances seldom
deter them, for when they search, they can always find other options.
The constant threat of violence swirling around them only increases
their ability to see the energy that opposition can engender as a
woman lives her personal vision of peace.

Here, then, are the extraordinary lives of twelve women of Jerusalem who have made their home in this city of perpetual war—and learned to make their own peace.

Notes

1. A muezzin is an Islamic official who calls the faithful to prayer.
2. A shofar is a ram's horn blown like a trumpet on special Jewish holidays.
3. Zatar is a golden, currylike mixture of spices that is uniquely Middle Eastern.
4. *Nebi* in Arabic and *Naveh* in Hebrew means "prophet."
5. Individuals living in occupied land—or the territories, as they are called—were required to have blue license plates at that time.
6. Carol Lynn Pearson, "The Woman," *The Search* (Provo, Utah: Trilogy Arts, 1970), 25.

2. BERTHA SPAFFORD VESTER

I can remember lying awake in the early morning, when the first glimmerings of light outlined my windows, and listening to the pit-a-pit, pit-a-pit of the unshod hooves of a donkey as it led a long caravan of camels through the street outside. Then came the soft shuffling footfalls of the camels and the rhythmic sighing of the ropes that fastened heavy loads to saddles, as the caravan plodded toward the market. That was [in 1881]. I was three years old, and my parents had just brought me to live in Jerusalem, the Holy City that was to become the only home I have ever known.[1]

Bertha Spafford Vester

I first encountered Bertha Spafford Vester in a little book of her water-colors celebrating the wildflowers of the Holy Land. Her lovely face on the book jacket enthralled me. That she directed a hospital for children of all races impressed me. Some referred to her as the "Mother of Jerusalem." She was a legend in her own time.

A friend had given me this little book as I prepared for my first trip to the Holy Land, to encourage me to stop to see the flowers. Little did I know the quest I was beginning or what beauty I would find beyond the flowers.

When I realized that our journey in the summer of 1968 would include Jerusalem, I was determined to meet Mrs. Vester in person. Her eminence didn't deter me; I am the kind of person who always makes an effort to meet the people I admire. There is so much more to be learned up close than at a distance. On our arrival, I phoned for an appointment.

Mrs. Vester's daughter, Anna Grace Lind, said that her mother always greeted visitors on Sunday afternoons in the garden of the American Colony Hotel, where she lived. We would be welcome there that afternoon. Happily, the three of us—I, my husband and a doctor from Seattle who was traveling with us—were the only visitors on that sunny afternoon. We had her all to ourselves.

As I have studied her life since, how I wish I had asked her a long list of questions. But on that day I had barely arrived. Jerusalem seemed strange and a bit forbidding. In time one discovers the incredible warmth and hospitality of all of its citizens—Arab, Jew, and Christian. But at the time, I knew only what the average novice tourist would know of the legendary city. One must study Jerusalem over time, not just glimpse it, to begin to sense its history. And here was Bertha Spafford Vester, whose life had spanned nearly a century of its recent stormy story. She was a veritable repository of that history.

The short entry in my journal for Sunday, June 9, 1968, reads:

Next to visit Mrs. Bertha Spafford Vester, 90 yr. old American at the American Colony Hotel. Lovely lady. She said the reason she had gotten on so well with Jew and Arab and Turk and English

*was because she was a Christian. 84 years she has lived in
Jerusalem. She said, "I have seen history."*

As the sun set that Sunday I wrote my impressions of her:

> *Mrs. Vester in her garden at vespers,*
> *Outshining her flowers.*
> *A Christian, having little problem*
> *With Turk or Arab or Jew,*
> *A vibrant love,*
> *Alive and wise at 90.*
> *Lover of the little . . .*
> *Flowers, babies.*
> *So sensible*
> *She found the small to prize.*

My assessment of this gracious American, who had lived her entire
life in Jerusalem, was that she was a strong, beautiful woman who had
always used all the resources at her disposal to do what she perceived
needed doing. She was a great lady with tangible presence. Obviously
a woman of enormous talent, she nevertheless seemed hardly conscious of herself. Perhaps at ninety one is better able to forget oneself.
I was impressed by her vitality at age ninety, but since then, from her
own words, I have glimpsed a younger, even more vigorous woman.

Bertha Spafford Vester died within days of our visit; we read of
her death as we toured Lebanon. How I cherish our visit in her garden that day, which contained what she referred to as the "one small
patch of lawn in all Jerusalem." Only a year after the dust and dirt of
the Six Day War, her garden was one of the few spots of color in a
newly united Jerusalem. I don't recall seeing any other garden in the
city on that trip. Her Jerusalem was a drab, dusty place. No wonder
she chose to plant and paint bright, lovely flowers!

She was a natural botanist and lover of nature, a watercolor artist
with an eye for beauty. Later I learned in her own words of her first experience in an American wood on a family vacation in the Adirondacks.

It was the first time in my life I had been part of the woods. I loved the woodsy smell, the soft, mossy, and narrow paths cut through the trees, and the wild flowers which were strange to me. The American buttercups are graceful, as compared to our Palestinian buttercups, which have thick, stiff stems.[2]

I discovered a book she had written, called *Our Jerusalem.* Since it was largely autobiographical, I wondered at first why she hadn't called it *My Jerusalem,* but by the time I laid the book down, I knew why. The American Colony community she described was exactly that, a community. She became its leading force after her mother, Anna Spafford, died.

Anna pioneered the Colony's humanitarian causes. Bertha never saw herself apart from the tasks her mother and father had begun when they came to Jerusalem in 1881. Even her marriage in 1904 to a young German businessman also reared in the tradition of Christian service (his parents were German Lutheran missionaries) was a continuation of her parents' covenant. Her determination to continue that service without stint was a legacy inherited by her own daughter, Anna Grace Lind.

These three generations of Jerusalem women have served the needy of that city through the hunger and pain of war from 1881 to our own time. Their lives were their message, touching the lives of other women and inspiring them to take up the tasks these matriarchs pioneered. Bertha recorded that around 1900, Anna, the first of the three, wrote to a supporter:

Our family [meaning the Colony] is very large. Many times larger than it ever was before, and consequently my cares are much greater. We number about one hundred and thirty, and forty of this number are children.

The Mohammedans [Muslims] and Jews are most kind to us. When we arrived back from the United States [where she had been to collect funds to continue the venture] one of them gave us a horse, another killed a cow and sent us the whole of it. Others

Members of the American colony assemble, c. 1908, outside their Ottoman villa. Founder Anna Spafford is seated, second from left, in the second row; daughter Bertha Spafford Vester holds a baby, far right; blond grandchild Anna Grace sits on a blanket, front right.

sent us bags of rice and charcoal. Another gave us olives from twenty-seven trees. These olives we have pickled and put up for the winter. Where we can, we return their kindness. We nurse their sick and teach their children. There are many ways in which we can help them.[3]

How understated Anna was in describing the gigantic task her family had undertaken. Anna left a living legacy of peace through service.

Her daughter Bertha's book is filled with matter-of-fact accounts of superhuman efforts. The following is but one example, taken from a letter written in 1917 before the United States had entered World War I. Conditions in Jerusalem were deteriorating daily, mostly because of the war. That same winter, 1917, Palestine had the worst locust infestation in generations and produced little grain. A Mr. Loud had sent money, and Anna wrote to thank him for his help:

If you could stand one day at our gate, and see the pleasure on the gaunt faces, as they go away with their pails and saucepans filled with the nutritious soup, enough to satisfy their family, it would repay you for your trouble. When I last wrote we were giving soup to four hundred people daily. Since then we have every day been obliged to increase the number, until Saturday (day before yesterday) there were eleven hundred and eighty-six souls who were fed. All the last week there were from nine hundred to one thousand daily. Working among the poor as we have, in and around Jerusalem for so many years, we get to know them all personally. However, we are cautious about accepting new applicants, and several of the sisters make it their duty to visit the homes and see exactly what they need. The deplorable condition of these homes is shocking. Americans cannot conceive, even by trying to imagine, what the reality is. . . .

. . . Some may think it would be wiser to limit the number of recipients and thus make the money last longer. This one could only advise from a distance where you do not see the applicants. It is utterly impossible to refuse.[4]

In another letter Anna confides her concern for the children:

It is the babies and children who suffer. They have had no part in bringing about this sad state of affairs. Their appealing glances would break hearts of stone. . . .

We make no distinction in nationality or creed, the only requirement being if they absolutely need the help. We have Syrians and Arabs, both Mohammedans, Latins and Greeks [referring to Christian religious denominations], and Armenians, Russians, Jews, and Protestants.[5]

This universal outreach explained Bertha's comment to me about her peaceful coexistence with the many occupiers of Jerusalem. Her determination was to serve any who were in need, regardless of race or religion. The American Colony was a peaceful island, no matter what conflicts swirled around it.

Bertha was three years old when her family settled in Jerusalem. The city was then held by the Ottoman Turks, who had ruled the region for nearly four hundred years. A little more than three decades later, she watched as Jerusalem became embroiled in World War I. At the end of that war, the British Mandate commenced, and the British began setting things to rights, putting the city back together as the Turks retreated. Between 1936 and 1939, the Arab Rebellion colored life in Jerusalem, bringing strikes and an Intifada long before the more recent ones.[6]

On the heels of that rebellion came World War II and the intrigues of Hitler's plans for Africa and the Middle East. At the end of that war, the liberation of the death camps freed thousands of Jews, who chose to settle in their promised land, later called Israel. In 1948, the Jewish War of Independence brought part of Jerusalem under Israeli jurisdiction.

The complexion of the land changed with the influx of three million Jews over the next few years. In 1968, the Six Day War brought the whole Jordanian West Bank, including a now united Jerusalem, under Israeli control. Living constantly in these conditions of war, the

The West Bank (the backward "B"), 1967

American Colony, led first by Anna and then by Bertha, responded to the hungry, the wounded, the homeless, and the families of the dead. Bertha had indeed seen history.

One of Bertha's memories was how, at the onset of World War I, during a period of hunger and deprivation, the American Colony managed to produce the vast amounts of soup they fed to the needy:

> We borrowed from the Armenian Convent the large copper cauldrons they used to cook food for their pilgrims during the pilgrimage season. We started cooking the soup about five in the morning and refilled the large cauldrons several times. I wrote to Mr. Loud:
>
> "It shows the increase in poverty, when last year the Jews would not take our cooked soup, but asked for the uncooked cereals [undoubtedly to keep kosher] while this year they are eager and grateful to get it."[7]

World War I drew closer, and the Germans closed the soup kitchen, claiming it was American propaganda.

Early in April 1917, citizens of Jerusalem feared that the city would become a battlefield again, as it had been on countless occasions throughout history. Americans were advised to leave, hopefully to return after Allied powers had helped win the fight. Bertha, in characteristic understatement, recalls, "A retreating Turkish army would be an unpleasant thing to encounter." Anna Spafford asked the American Embassy officials if they were being ordered to leave. She was told that Americans don't order their citizens to do anything, but they were strongly advised to leave. Bertha remembers:

Mother thought a moment and then answered that as she had left her country to be of service to the people of Palestine, she considered this her supreme hour for service; as far as she was concerned she would not leave. The whole Colony confirmed this decision; not one left.[8]

One must remember that the Colony was made up mostly of Americans, and that as a result they were not inconspicuous.[9]

On April 6 [1917] the United States declared war on the German Reich. The inevitable breaking off of diplomatic relations with Turkey came as a matter of course, although the United States never actually declared war on Turkey, a fact we hoped would make conditions easier for us in the American Colony.[10]

The British unsuccessfully attacked Gaza, and the prisoners taken by the Turks, together with many wounded on both sides, were brought to Jerusalem and paraded through the streets. Stretchers lined the road outside the French Hospital, and the Spaffords and others in the American Colony nursed the wounded from both sides.

Bertha's vigor and vision reflected her mother's. She observes: "The atmosphere of the Colony was happy, the aura reverential and devout. Need was the incentive that put every bit of accumulated knowledge to work and every talent to use."[11]

The strife of war provided a continuous backdrop for the Colony's labor. Though the city knew periods of relative peace, the longest of which may have been the thirty years during the British Mandate (1918 to 1948), at many other times the inhabitants of the Colony witnessed carnage, hunger, and death. How senseless it must have seemed to them, whether watching from the sidelines or in the very center of the battle, as Arabs, Jews, Turks, British, Germans, and others by turn fought over Jerusalem.

When the occupation of the city by the British began, Bertha, by then forty years old, wanted to help but was not certain what to do:

The British Mandate had a colossal job on its hands. They needed help, but what should that be? Certainly not something they, in their official capacity, could do better than we.

It must be something they would or could not do, and that work, we decided, could be done by the women of Jerusalem.[12]

Bertha determined that she should educate the city's young Arab girls, thus lifting their sights above the menial tasks to which they were accustomed. Perhaps she drew upon her own earlier experience:

When I was in my teens, my father had a great friend, Ismail Bey, a leading [Arab] citizen. The two spent hours discussing the country's affairs and how conditions could be improved.

They agreed that Arab women must be better educated. When Ismail Bey became minister of education, he was interested in a school for Moslem girls, then limited to instruction in the Koran. Ismail Bey asked the American Colony to provide a headmistress.

I volunteered, but since I was only eighteen, my mother said I was too young. I suggested my governess, Miss Brooke. Too old, said Mother. Then it was decided that Miss Brooke and I would share the job. Her experience would balance my knowledge of Arabic.

The school was established near the Dome of the Rock, in the Moslem quarter.

Again, there was difficulty about pronouncing my name. The nearest the girls could get to it was Bursa, which in Arabic means leper—and I certainly didn't want to be called that! A friend suggested that we solve the problem by giving me an Arabic name.

"Why not take my wife's name—Afifi?" he said. So I became Sitt (Lady) Afifi.[13]

That experience prepared her for expanding education for girls in Jerusalem during the British Mandate. It had been more than twenty years since those students had called her Sitt Afifi. She had already established a small industrial school, and when the British arrived after the war, she enlarged it:

I have already mentioned the starting of the Industrial School during the early years of the war [World War I]. Now we enlarged the school and added plain sewing and dressmaking classes. Instruction was given in the three R's [reading, writing and arithmetic] in Arabic, and English was taught. Needle lace and embroidery, using traditional patterns characteristic to the country, were developed. Later we added knitting, crocheting, and weaving.[14]

Although her early training enhanced her work in education, lack of training in other areas didn't deter her from providing aid. Tutored only by necessity, she nursed the sick and the many wounded of the wars she lived through. This, of course, was in addition to caring for her own six children and her husband. Very early, Jerusalem's children of all races and nationalities, many of them orphans, became her special concern.

In 1925, Bertha Spafford Vester established the Spafford Children's Center in the Old City of Jerusalem, named in honor of her mother, who had died on April 17, 1923, and who in her day had also reached out to the babies of Jerusalem.[15] On Christmas Eve in the year of her mother's passing, Bertha met a woman in great need of medical help:

> As I was hurrying down the hill leading from the school, I met a woman coming up. She was being helped on one side by a man and on the other by an elderly woman. This woman was carrying a bundle of filthy rags. I saw at once that the woman who was being helped was very sick. I stopped and asked them where they were going.
>
> The man answered, "Allah knows!"
>
> I peeked into the bundle and found it contained a wee baby only a few days old.
>
> I said, "Your wife is very sick."
>
> "I know it," he replied. "I brought her for six hours on donkey-back to the hospital only to find it closed to out patients because they said you had a feast today."
>
> I was greatly touched. I thought as I stood beside the mother and child that I was rushing off to sing carols in the shepherds' fields to commemorate the birth of a babe who was born in a stable and placed in a manger because there was no room in the inn, and here before me stood a rustic Madonna and babe, and, metaphorically speaking, [there was] no room for them in the inn.[16]

Mrs. Vester acted immediately. The family was admitted to the hospital, but by morning the mother had died. The distraught father carried the baby back to Mrs. Vester and implored her to take his little son, as he lived in a cave and there was no one to look after the child. Baby Noel (as he was later named) was the first child in the Baby Home Bertha established.

The orphanage grew into a children's hospital and served the surrounding area until 1967, when the reunification of Jerusalem under Israeli rule made better-equipped hospitals available. At that point, the staff of the Spafford Center decided to focus on prenatal care, edu-

The Old House viewed from the North

cation and preventive medicine. Though Bertha lived to be part of this change, she died the next year.

The Spafford Center continues to serve the mothers and babies of Jerusalem. It is housed in the original Spafford family home near the northern wall of the Old City, a spot easily seen from a point overlooking the Place of the Skull inside the Garden Tomb enclave.

Bertha's response in helping others meet adversity was direct and immediate—a response shaped by personal experience with adversity. She was a woman of great faith, great hope, and an indomitable will to make the things happen for which she prayed. Here, she chronicles one of the trials of her faith.

It was just before Christmas, that first year of the war [World War I]. We had no electricity, no kerosene, and candles were very scarce. We reverted to the Biblical lamps like those used by the wise and unwise virgins, only ours were improvised out of sardine tins with two holes, one for the wick and one for oil, and filled with sesame oil. Frederick and I had five children at this time and no way of buying anything to make Christmas seem usual and normal. So I was making Christmas presents out of odds and ends.

Tanetta had come back from school that afternoon flushed and hot. I soaked her feet in a hot mustard bath and put her to bed. I was sewing on some dolls' clothes, keeping very close to the wick of the lamp. Frederick was near me and was reading Dickens's Christmas Carol *aloud. We were trying hard to get into the Christmas spirit when the nurse came down to say that she feared Tanetta was very ill. She was exceedingly hot and seemed delirious. The thermometer showed that her fever was as high as it could possibly go; I knew it could not go much higher and she still live, but what alarmed me most was that she was cold up to her knees.*[17]

When the doctor confirmed that Tanetta was ill with either spotted typhus or smallpox, they knew they must quarantine at once.

Our four remaining children were awakened, dressed, and taken over to the Colony [just three minutes away, where Bertha's mother, Anna Spafford, would care for them]. I stayed to nurse Tanetta. The plan was for Frederick to remain downstairs in our house and be the liaison between me and the outside world. The worst fear—anguish beyond words—was that the Turkish sanitary authorities would take our child away to the pesthouse, from which she would not return. . . .

It was soon certain that she had a bad attack of smallpox. . . .

No one else in the Colony caught the infection, and we were a united family for Christmas, which was the best present we could have been given.[18]

Tanetta's recovery affirmed Bertha's already firm belief in God. That faith was severely tested a short time later when her husband, Frederick, and son John were taken seriously ill with what they called typhoid malaria. She was then pregnant with her sixth child. One day, the doctor took her aside during the vigil she was keeping over her husband and son. He was convinced that Frederick's heart was failing and that he would soon die. Bertha writes:

When the doctor left I went into the library. Mother was there. I must have looked utterly dejected and hopeless. Mother did not know what the doctor had told me, but she came over and looked into my face.

"Bertha," she asked in her deep, wonderful voice, "is God dead?"

"No, Mother," I answered, "God is not dead."

Remembering that, I went out into the garden. I do not know how long I was there; I lost count of time. Suddenly the window of my husband's sickroom opened and Sister Lottie spoke to me. "Your husband is asking for you."

Frederick was conscious for the first time in days.

He grew rapidly better, John's fever turned, and both were quite recovered when two months later Frieda, our youngest, was born. Although I had passed through sore trials and had insufficient food, Frieda is one of the healthiest and happiest of our six children.[19]

Christmas as celebrated by Bertha in Jerusalem was remembered by many who were blessed by her Christmas spirit.

On Christmas Eve, 1925, we had given the girls of the School of Handicrafts and Dressmaking a jolly tea party, with plenty of cake, candy and oranges, and a Christmas tree and presents followed by games.

It was over and the girls had gone off in a happy mood. I was joining my husband and the children to sing carols on the shepherds' fields near Bethlehem. It was the first time this had been done. It happened to be a full moon, and the weather, which is often wet and cold at Christmastime, was pleasant. . . .

. . . Imagine the thrill it gave one to be singing carols on the shepherds' fields, with stars brilliant overhead as they are in that dry climate, and looking up to Bethlehem in the distance and seeing the lights flickering in that hallowed place!

I had been asked to lead the singing, and accepted with pleasure.[20]

Bertha tells of other Christmases, too. Some, in wartime, were barely celebrated. But always there was a thrill at celebrating the sacred Christian season in Jerusalem. Her mother saw to it that Christmas was celebrated, whatever their circumstances.

Anna Spafford describes the family's first Christmas in Jerusalem in a letter dated January 6, 1882: "Our Christmas was a very quiet one and did not seem a bit like those at home, as there was nothing to remind us of it."

But in 1885, three years later, Anna wrote:

Christmas! Glorious rain all night. [December is the normal time for the rainy season in biblical and modern times.] Fifty-two outsiders here during the afternoon and evening. The tree beautifully trimmed, supper served to young and old. Thirty-two outside our "family" received gifts from the tree. The most wonderful peace and order combined with joy filled the house.[21]

Another description of Christmas celebrations includes a list of gifts from their Muslim Arab friends. Bertha described some of the gifts as:

payments in kind for the education of their [the Arabs'] children and for nursing their sick; [while] others were simply Christmas presents.

Ahmed Offendi sent a sheep; Sheik Mohammed a basket of rice, the same came from the Mayor of Jerusalem, two turkeys from Hussain, two ducks and two geese and four baskets of oranges from Faidi Effendi al Alami. From others (I can't remember the names) we got four trays of "buklaway" [baklava] (Arabic sweetmeat), one tray of geribi (like Scotch shortbread), one tray of "mamoul."[22]

Sundays were also days for celebration. The young people at the American Colony had a choir and band and organized themselves into an art and literary club. Each Sunday afternoon there was a religious service at 3 P.M. and afterwards a social hour in which the band played, the choir sang and refreshments were served, usually tea, coffee and coffee bread. On many of those Sunday afternoons, thirty or forty people would visit the Colony, especially during the tourist season. They would sing hymns until the lamps were lighted, and many remained for supper.

It became evident to me, in retrospect, why Bertha Spafford Vester preserved the Sunday afternoon tradition of meeting friends, even strangers or tourists like myself. And it explains why, to my surprise and delight, Anna Grace Lind didn't hesitate to invite us to visit her mother on that sunny Sunday afternoon in 1968.

Others have shared with me their memories of Bertha. Mary Franji, the head nurse at the Spafford Center, was surprised to have been hired by her:

> *They told me Mrs. Vester needed a nurse at the Spafford. But I had nursed her at the English Hospital once when she had pneumonia and typhoid. She was very sick. She didn't like me much because I was small and there was a German Jewess who was large and comfortable looking. [She liked her.]*
>
> *So when I went to see her for the job I told her, "Maybe you don't remember me but you never liked me. You always said, 'Let this nurse stay. Mary, you go.'" Then she said, "If you are from the English Mission Hospital, I must like you. And I don't want to see any references. The nurses there are good nurses." Then she said to me, "You must always say, 'I'm small but good!'" Later, when she would pass by me at the Spafford, she would say, "Oh, Mary, you're there, my little nurse."[23]*

Mary went on to tell me how it was with Bertha as she aged and couldn't walk up the hill to the Spafford Center:

> *Later on, when she was getting old, she couldn't get here so she came on a donkey. And the children were all clapping, seeing an old woman on a donkey that was a little awkward. Then she changed to a wheel chair and she had to be pushed to come.*

I must say she was wonderful, she never gave up until she couldn't come anymore. The people liked her very much. They knew that she was the one who really helped them. .

In these later memories, Mary was describing the Bertha I had met. I had not known about the donkey or the wheelchair, but it didn't surprise me.

When I asked Hind Husseini, one of the Arab girls she had mothered, what she remembered of Bertha Spafford Vester, Hind replied:

She was handsome, with really beautiful features, and she was tall. She had a very graceful body and a smiling face, always. Her sister [Mrs. Whiting] was very nice also but a different style. She [Bertha] was maybe the most beautiful person in Jerusalem, a real lady.

She was a wonderful woman. I not only liked her, I was impressed by her.

I attended her husband's funeral and her funeral and they were buried in the American cemetery up on the Mount of Olives. They were the last to be buried there. After her husband died she prepared her grave beside her husband and she was buried there.

All Jerusalem went to her funeral. Her husband's funeral was in the winter and the streets were full of snow but still everybody followed the funeral. They liked them.

They found that they were really good people, this American Colony group. They were opening small clinics and the baby home in the Old City and they became very friendly with them and even she [Bertha] was enrolled to work with my Uncle Ismail Bey. He was the director of education and took her as a teacher and advisor in the women's schools. They were very much impressed by her. Mrs. Vester was a personality![24]

Everyone who lived in Jerusalem during the time of Bertha Spafford Vester knew her. It was a relatively small town in those days. She was at Jerusalem's social center, invited to receptions and hosting many herself at the Colony. During one such event at which she was the hostess in 1941, the famous General Allenby paid tribute to her, after she had "introduced His Lordship to the many friends gathered to meet him."

> *You have just listened to Mrs. Vester's thrilling and gallant speech, spoken, I must say, with great modesty. I hardly know what to say after that.*
>
> *I recall the time within these walls when I had the privilege of meeting Mrs. Spafford [Bertha's mother]. The important work that she and her husband began over fifty years ago has been loyally carried on by her daughters. America has indeed reason to be proud of such citizens as Mrs. Spafford and her two daughters, Mrs. Vester [Bertha] and Mrs. Whiting [Grace].*
>
> *The important work for the youth of this land is being done by the American Colony. The care of neglected and badly nourished babies, the teaching of mothers to care for, clothe, and feed their babies in the proper manner, the training of young girls in the simple but most essential household arts, are a great work, I say, and most nobly done.*[25]

Others have praised her in print. In 1962, when Bertha was eighty-four, her longtime friend, Lowell Thomas wrote of her:

> *She has known kings, princes, field marshals—and thousands of humble people, Muslims, Jews and Christians who call her simply "Ummuna." In Arabic that is "mother of us all."*
>
> *What has Bertha Vester done? What hasn't she done! As a child, she was formally adopted by an Arab tribe. Once she mercifully amputated a Turkish soldier's arms (although she hadn't the slightest medical training). It was she who furnished the white surrender flag used when Jerusalem fell to the British in 1917—a part of a hospital sheet! She stoutly faced death in heavy gunfire during the fierce battles of 1948.*
>
> *A gifted painter of Palestine's wildflowers, she has also written a book called* Our Jerusalem. *She speaks a bewildering num-*

ber of languages, including perfect Arabic. Above all, she has
devoted her life to Jerusalem's babies and children—teaching
them, caring for them.[26]

Those are the very lines that invited me to learn more about
Bertha Spafford Vester and sent me to the American Colony to meet
her in 1968. What blessed serendipity!

Bertha loved Jerusalem and Jerusalem returned that love. One
day as I walked up the hill to the Spafford Home with her daughter,
Anna Grace, who was then eighty-eight, a little Arab woman stopped
her, calling her, "Umama Yerusalem" ("Mother of Jerusalem").

Afterwards I commented, "Didn't she call you 'Mother of
Jerusalem?'"

"Yes," she replied, "but I'm not."

"Isn't that what they called your mother?" I asked.

"Oh yes," she smiled, "but she was."

Notes

1. Bertha Spafford Vester, "Jerusalem, My Home," *National Geographic,* December
    1964, 826.
2. Bertha Spafford Vester, *Our Jerusalem* (Jerusalem: Ariel Publishing House, 1988),
    339–40.
3. Vester, *Our Jerusalem,* 189.
4. Vester, *Our Jerusalem,* 257.
5. Vester, *Our Jerusalem,* 257–58.
6. This Intifada took place in the 1930s. Another began in December 1987 and con-
    tinued until the peace process began in 1993. The Intifada that began in 2000
    continues to the present day.
7. Vester, *Our Jerusalem,* 258.
8. Vester, *Our Jerusalem,* 259.
9. In August 1896, the Americans had been joined by a group of thirty-eight
    Swedish farmers, including seventeen children, one of whom was a babe in arms.
10. Vester, *Our Jerusalem,* 259.
11. Vester, *Our Jerusalem,* 189.
12. Vester, *Our Jerusalem,* 326.

13. Vester, "Jerusalem, My Home," 833–34. Ismeil Bey was Hind Husseini's uncle (see chapter on Hind Husseini). The Koran is the Muslim holy book.

14. Vester, *Our Jerusalem,* 326. One wonders if this program was a forerunner of Sahir Dajani's project sponsored by the Mennonites to help local women maintain their embroidery skills and market their products. See chapter on Sahir Alami Dajani.

15. Vester, *Our Jerusalem,* 310.

16. Vester, *Our Jerusalem,* 327.

17. Vester, *Our Jerusalem,* 252.

18. Vester, *Our Jerusalem,* 253.

19. Vester, *Our Jerusalem,* 254.

20. Vester, *Our Jerusalem,* 326–27. This celebration was the one described to me by Hind Husseini as one of her earliest, happiest memories. See also the chapters on Anna Grace Lind, Hind Husseini and Mary Franji.

21. Vester, *Our Jerusalem,* 72.

22. Vester, *Our Jerusalem,* 191–92.

23. See the chapter on Mary Franji.

24. See the chapter on Hind Husseini.

25. Vester, *Our Jerusalem,* 342.

26. Bertha Spafford Vester, *Flowers of the Holy Land* (Kansas, Mo.: Hallmark Cards, 1966), 12.

3. ANNA GRACE LIND

Arabs and Jews are so alike. They don't realize how alike they are. I told them about Ezekiel 47. The land must be shared with the people of the land. I wrote Mr. Baker [James Baker, U. S. Secretary of State at the time] and told him this. [Sharing the land] is my solution to the Arab-Israeli conflict. I told him he was doing a wonderful job.

Anna Grace Vester Lind

Writing the American Secretary of State to offer her advice was standard operating procedure for Anna Grace Lind.[1] Why not give him the benefit of her hard-earned wisdom? He hadn't lived in Jerusalem. She had lived there for a very long time. Why not offer help to someone with the power to change things?

Anna Grace Vester Lind was eighty-seven years old when I interviewed her in Jerusalem. She had only recently relinquished the management of "the Spafford" (the Spafford Children's Center), which her mother had established in 1925, to a group that she hoped would carry on the work her family had started. She had no daughter to call home to Jerusalem as her mother had called her forty-four years before.

Anna Grace met me for lunch at the American Colony Hotel nearly twenty-five years after our first meeting on the day I visited her mother, Bertha Spafford Vester. Anna Grace had spoken very little on that summer day in 1968, allowing me the freedom to speak directly with her mother. Often, adult children of aged parents answer for them as if they were not present, but Anna Grace showed no such tendency. In fact, she deferred to her ninety-year-old mother even when we directed questions to Anna Grace herself. I understood this better now. Everyone, I had learned, deferred to Bertha Spafford Vester.

The day of our second meeting, in 1992, was a lovely spring day in Jerusalem after the hardest winter in a hundred years. We had a pleasant lunch served in the garden court of the American Colony Hotel, not far from the very spot where we had first met a quarter of a century before. Across the courtyard from us grew a palm tree, one of a pair given to Anna Grace's mother and father as wedding gifts by Baron Ustinov, grandfather of Peter Ustinov. The other of the pair had been a casualty of the shelling of this courtyard during the 1948 war.

Anna Grace was a small woman with gray hair cropped short. Her gray-blue eyes flashed when she was exercised about something, which she often was. She was clean and neatly dressed, not an easy task in dusty Jerusalem or at her advanced age. Her only jewelry was a long strand of large amber beads she wore on nearly every occasion.

Her memory served her well. It was almost like watching an animated history, listening to her recollections of growing up in Jerusalem.

Born in Jerusalem on February 3, 1905, Anna Grace had many memories of her childhood. The young Anna Grace was well aware of her mother's philanthropies, and obviously saw Mrs. Vester as a good and caring mother to many beyond her own family. One might have wondered, though, whether this great lady's many charities had left her children, at least her eldest daughter, feeling left out sometimes. Anna Grace details one vivid memory:

Just before Jerusalem was surrendered to the British and Lord Allenby came into the city on December 11, 1917, there was a lot of fighting going on north of the American Colony. Mother was very busy nursing the wounded, and our nanny was quite old and confused by all the fighting. Of course, my brother Horatio and I were interested in all the excitement and the fighting so we sneaked out and went to follow the army. [They would have been ten and twelve years old at the time.]

We got to the place north of the city where there had been a big battle, and we found dead soldiers lying all around. Their guns and hand grenades—all their weapons—were just lying on the ground, so we had a field day! We loaded our pockets with grenades and slung as many rifles as we could over our shoulders, adding ammunition to our bulging pockets.

As you can imagine, when Mother returned home and found us missing, she was very worried and organized a search party to look for us. The search party found us just at dusk on the outskirts of Jerusalem. At first they thought we were Turkish soldiers, because of the rifles on our shoulders, but then they recognized us and took us home. Mother and Father were there to meet us, and Father stripped us of our weapons, taking all the rifles and hand grenades and emptying our pockets. But I had sneaked one hand grenade and had hidden it, and Father didn't find it.

Horatio and I were sent up to the nursery in disgrace, and then I showed him the hand grenade I had hidden. He told me that the only thing that made a hand grenade dangerous was the gunpowder inside, and that if you took out the screw at the bot-

Anna Grace on the right at the end

*tom of the grenade and let out the gunpowder, it would be quite
harmless. Horatio proceeded to show me and took out the screw,
emptying the powder over the nursery wood burning stove! The
whole stove exploded and the room was filled with smoke!
Mother and Father came rushing upstairs and were greeted by
this terrible mess. We were unhurt, but you can be sure that we
had our punishment.*[2]

On a later visit, Anna Grace asked about news accounts of violence in the United States. I suggested that some of it could be connected with the violence seen on television by children. She said
incredulously, "You mean that they encourage this sort of thing?" Her
concern was real. She had lived with violence.

Her childhood, though punctuated by war, had tranquil aspects.
Her relationship with her maternal grandmother, Anna Spafford, was
an important influence in those years. Anna Grace adored her grandmother, for whom she had been named. Often, inheriting a name pro-

duces a unique connection with that person. Georgette Lind, wife of Anna Grace's son Peter, remembers:

> *On one of our visits to Jerusalem, [Peter and I] were given a lovely, spacious room downstairs in the Colony. It opened off the courtyard. Anna Grace came to welcome us and she stood in the doorway, smiling and happy, and telling us that our room had been her grandmother Anna's room. "This was my grandmother's room, and I loved coming here often to talk with her."*
>
> *She would tell me every day how much she had enjoyed her visits with her grandmother in that room and what a special part she had played in her life.*
>
> *Anna Grace visited us far more on that occasion and was the most relaxed I had seen her. Whether it was because the surroundings created an aura of security for her or not, we'll never know. It could have been just a tranquil time for her. She never stopped mentioning that we were in her grandmother's room.*

Anna Grace spoke of many Jerusalem memories in her long and eventful life. Which did she remember most fondly? After only a moment's thought, she says, "The British Mandate." She was thirteen years old when the British first occupied Jerusalem and forty-three when they left: "The young Britishers mixed with the young people of the town, and we had wonderful fun—dances and picnics."

Her face shone as she remembered. She painted a picture one would never have guessed existed had she not lived it. The British Mandate is not always happily remembered in Israel. But a pretty young girl, born to an American mother and a German father and reared in Jerusalem, thought of it as the happiest of times. It was a time of relative peace, a rarity in this ancient city.

Anna Grace, who was constantly reading, devouring all kinds of literature, attended school in Jerusalem. Her earliest school was in the American Colony, but after the British came, she attended an Anglican school, a descendant of which still operates in Jerusalem and sets a high standard of education in the city. Her brothers were sent to boarding schools in America. Her parents cared deeply about the education of their children.

She spoke of her mother's knowing Arabic well but insisting that her children not learn it because she feared their being considered "Levantine."[3]

> *But I know kitchen Arabic. . . . We picked it up from the servants. I once went to an Ulpan [a Hebrew intensive language training] at the Sisters of Zion to learn Hebrew, but all the other students were Palestinians and picked it up quickly. I soon gave it up. Of course I understand much that is said.*

Before our interview, as we were walking through the American Colony dining room, Anna Grace had told me that her Arabic was minimal. Hearing this, a nearby Palestinian waiter winked at me behind her back and said aloud, "She is our teacher! Mrs. Lind could be *your* teacher. She knows very well." She laughed and said, "Why, thank you," very quietly, almost shyly.

Anna Grace met her future husband in the American Colony. Nils Erickson Lind was one of the Swedish members of the Colony and twelve years older than Anna Grace. The young girl's mother, Mrs. Vester, had had a falling-out with one of the Swedes in the Colony, and the marriage of her oldest daughter may have been an alliance to make peace. It would not be farfetched to call it an "arranged marriage," in the tradition of the Middle East. The couple were married in 1925 when Anna Grace was nineteen and Nils was thirty-one.

They lived in Jerusalem for a time but soon moved to New York City, where they ran an import-export business for the American Colony. Their wares were oriental rugs, olivewood carvings and postcards made from photos that originated in the American Colony photo shop. These came to be known as the Mattson Collection, some of which still exist. During this time Anna Grace became the mother of two sons, Peter and Tony, both of whom are still living.[4]

Anna Grace told me very little of her life in America. Perhaps this was because America was the scene of her divorce. On that subject she said one day,

I had a friend who was going to Reno to get a divorce and asked me to go along. I went and while I was there it looked to be so easy to obtain a divorce that I got one myself. I hadn't thought it out. I was young and immature.

One surmises that the marriage had never felt like her own choice and that she had not found real happiness in it. On the only occasion we discussed it, she spoke of making rash decisions. Given time, she may have rethought that impulsive act. Her son Peter saw a good deal of his father, who lived in England, and obviously felt him to be a good man. Whether Anna Grace had had second thoughts, we can only guess.

At any rate, World War II had put an end to the American Colony import business when Hitler's U-boats made the shipping lanes in the Atlantic unsafe. Anna Grace went to Boston and worked for a time on Newbury Street in an interior design shop. She tried several vocations but never settled into one before returning to Jerusalem at her mother's request.

She speaks quite energetically about her stint in the U.S. Navy during World War II:

In New York City I was raising money for Bundles for Britain. It was funny how I got into the Navy. I was a single parent with two boys in boarding school. I needed money. I failed the [Navy] typing exam but was offered a job as Personnel Relations officer at Quonset Point.

Apparently, she gave up on the typing test after about five words but left a handwritten note on the typewriter outlining her qualifications and asking them to call if they could use her. They did.

I received two letters. The one said I'd failed the typing test. The other offered me a job as a personnel officer, and I became a Lt. Commander in the Navy.
Then in 1951, my mother asked me to come back to manage the [American Colony] Hotel, which I decided to do.

Anna Grace returned to Jerusalem, which she would call home until her death on December 3, 1994, just a few weeks short of her ninetieth birthday.

As longtime manager of the American Colony Hotel, she added comfort and convenience to a venue that had long been a popular gathering place in Jerusalem. A typically Middle Eastern building, its stone construction is mostly original, with a few modern sections added to expand occupancy. The renovating that Anna Grace did is the backbone of today's gracious hotel. The renovations included such ambitious projects as adding bathrooms in every room—there had only been two in the whole building before. She changed the entire hotel, taking advantage of the natural ambience of the former pasha's palace. It was a strenuous undertaking.

After she completed the project, she felt she needed a rest and, more than that, renewal. She spoke to her Anglican priest. He suggested the discipline of a convent, so she went to England to the Fairacres Convent at Oxford. At the end of a year, the Mother Superior told her flatly that she was not cut out to be a nun. However, Anna Grace seemed to believe that that year may have helped her accept herself as separate from her powerful mother. Perhaps it was indeed a year of renewal.

There were other times away from Jerusalem. Anna Grace lived off and on between 1959 and 1961 in Alabama with her son Peter and his wife, Georgette, and their two small sons, Eric and Brian. Georgette remembers that her mother-in-law was wonderful with the children, taking them for long walks in their buggy or stroller and telling them stories. Instead of calling her Grandmama they simply called her "Am." Georgette believes that the boys had learned to refer to their great-great-grandmother Anna Spafford as "Grandmama," probably because that was what Anna Grace would have called her in the stories she told them.

Her visit with Peter's family ended when her sister Frieda sent word that she was finding it difficult to be the only one helping their mother in the American Colony. Dutifully, Anna Grace returned to Jerusalem. But she visited Peter's family each summer in the United

States until her children worried that she was past the age to be able to travel alone. Then they visited her in Jerusalem.

All her life she had seen her mother creatively taking risks in dangerous circumstances, always living an exciting life. She had grown up in the larger-than-life shadow of her powerful mother—not an easy relationship. But her grandmother had mothered her in long-remembered ways. Anna Grace grew into an independent woman herself, in the pattern of both mother and grandmother.

As the hotel succeeded and her mother aged, Anna Grace turned her attention more and more to her mother's pet project, the Children's Center in the Old City. She explained:

Later Mother asked me to take over the Spafford Center, and I did. I lived at Spafford until December 1991 when I moved back over here to the Hotel.

The Spafford Children's Center, located on the north wall of the Old City, was in the original Spafford home, where her grandmother-namesake, Anna, had first settled in the city and where her mother, Bertha, had lived as a child. It is located on the top of a hill between Herod's Gate and the Damascus Gate.

For many years, Anna Grace lived in a quaint, comfortable apartment upstairs at the Spafford Children's Center, but the winter of 1991–92 abruptly thrust her out of the rhythm of her life. The open courtyard in her living quarters filled up with snow, and she had a difficult time moving from one room to another across that frigid space, which was dangerously icy.[5] Reluctantly, she moved a few blocks north to the American Colony Hotel.

No longer would Anna Grace need to carry her groceries to the top of the hill that had begun to seem rather steep. It would be more convenient to live at the American Colony. There she could depend on the services of the hotel, including excellent food. The staff at the Spafford Center and her family had joined in helping make the decision. But it was not a happy one for Anna Grace.

She hated feeling that her age curtailed or circumscribed her activities. And there were Spafford and Vester memories in every corner of that old stone house on the hill. One room contained antiques from an earlier era—photos, paintings, bric-a-brac and furniture, including a wonderful old desk built by hand for her father. Anna Grace used this room as an office. It was a repository of her family's history.

In early spring we walked up the hill together, but she left me to myself to wander through the upstairs rooms of her recently vacated apartment. The rooms surrounded the open courtyard with its flowering vines and giant red-orange geraniums, the largest I have ever seen. The apartment where she had lived until a few weeks before was still as she had left it. Of course, her paintings and most of her furniture were gone, but the ambience remained. Some of *her* remained. There were green plants and flowers everywhere.

The kitchen was well equipped but spartan, like most contemporary Jerusalem kitchens. Two nuns who were volunteering in the Center were now using the quarters. Their bedroom was starkly furnished, as if it were a monastery. They were cordial, but somehow I felt that we were all interlopers. I could picture those rooms furnished with Anna Grace's lovely antiques, which were now in her spacious apartment at the American Colony Hotel.

So much of Anna Grace's life had happened right here. There were innumerable memories. One singular event was recorded with typical reserve:

On the morning of June 5, 1967, Anna Grace, unaware that about two hours earlier the Israelis had made a pre-emptive air attack on Egypt, destroying virtually the whole Egyptian Air Force on the ground, was out in the hospital garden planting out some seedlings. When bullets began to hit the wall just above her head, she and her sister Frieda agreed that the war must indeed have begun. They decided to evacuate as many of the patients as possible before it was too late.

Thus began Anna Grace's experience of the Six Day War.

On Sunday, June 4, the American Colony was in Jordan. By the end of the week it was, de facto, in Israel.

While the Israelis were dancing in the streets of West Jerusalem to celebrate their amazing victory and the recapture of the city, it was a different picture in East Jerusalem. What to the Israelis was liberation and unification of the city was, to the majority of its Arab inhabitants, defeat, humiliation and foreign occupation. At the same time, there were many individual cases where Arabs and Jews who had been friends and neighbors before the partition were happy to be able to renew old ties, and there were emotional reunions across the "Green Line."[6]

I wondered why Anna Grace had sent me up alone to see the apartment where she had seen and experienced so much. I pictured the stone floor of the courtyard filling up with snow a few weeks before and the wrenching decision to leave what had been a treasured scene of her childhood as well as her chosen home as an adult. I concluded that the decision to move had been so painful for her that she now chose not to revisit her beloved rooms, even with a guest.

When I rejoined Anna Grace downstairs, she was reticent to speak of what I had just seen, so I changed the subject. As she showed me around the clinic, she spoke of her hope that this work would outlive her. The doctor and nurses there treated her with great respect and, even more important, with love. She and Mary Franji, head nurse at the Spafford, were obviously old and dear friends.

These were not her only friends in the neighborhood. That day as we had climbed up the hill to the Center, a small, older Arab woman, in traditional, brightly embroidered Palestinian dress, stopped Anna Grace, took her hand in hers and with shining eyes spoke to her animatedly in Arabic. Anna Grace answered her easily in Arabic, and they conversed amiably for several minutes.

When they bade each other goodbye with the usual *ma salaam,* I asked Anna Grace, "Didn't your friend keep calling you 'Mother of Jerusalem?'" She answered, "I'm really not. My mother was."

I smiled, because the present Arab population seems to hold another opinion.

We returned for tea to Anna Grace's lovely apartment in the American Colony. The walls, decorated with photos of her parents and paintings of her mother and grandmother, also displayed several of Bertha Spafford Vester's paintings of flowers and scenes in and around Jerusalem. Some of the furniture had come from her parents' household. Middle Eastern embroideries and carpets and flowers added to the ambience. The apartment had a lovely balcony where she said she sat during the times when it wasn't too hot or too cold. Everything felt comfortable and dignified.

Anna Grace spoke happily of managing the hotel when she first returned to Jerusalem, remembering the difficulties but now looking around her at the successful enterprise that she had helped to build. Then she spoke of her work with children at the Spafford Center. It had been her mother's pet project, and turning it over to her daughter signaled that Bertha recognized that she was aging.

During the Gulf War, Anna Grace spent her days inside the walls of the Old City at the Spafford Center, though she slept at the American Colony Hotel. It sounded risky. She remembers:

> It wasn't so bad during the Gulf War. We had a sealed room in the Colony. I felt safe at the Spafford during the day. Except at night. I didn't dare go by myself at night.[7]

"You are a strong woman," I said to this tiny lady. In one of our last conversations she told me her notion of how peace might finally come to Jerusalem and the Middle East:

> Two years ago when I was asked to speak to a group to tell the story of my grandparents Horatio and Anna Spafford, a young man asked, "What is your solution to the Arab-Israeli problem?"

In that speech she said she believed the Jews and Arabs are much alike, though neither group recognizes it. She felt that sharing the land made logical as well as biblical sense:

> Ezekiel 47 suddenly popped into my head. I thought it was inspiration. It reads: "You are to allot [this land] as an inheritance for

yourselves and for the aliens who have settled among you and who have children. You are to consider them as native-born Israelites; along with you they are to be allotted an inheritance among the tribes of Israel. In whatever tribe the alien settles, there you are to give him his inheritance, declares the Sovereign Lord" (NIV Ezekiel 47: 22–23).

The land must be shared with the people of the land. Arabs and Jews are so alike. They don't realize how alike they are. . . . This is my solution to the Arab-Israeli conflict . . . I suggested they share the land.

Does it sound too simple a solution? At nearly ninety years of age one tends to see the issues stripped down to their essential elements. This solution didn't come from an idle bystander, a weekend visitor, or a tourist who had become an instant expert by making a short visit. This solution came from one born in the city, one who was reared with Arab children and Jewish children before there was a Jewish state.

Her ideas have been forged in the crucible of war and real-life experience in this land and with these people. Proficiency in Arabic allowed her into a culture others can only skirt. Hers was a hands-on viewpoint, for she worked for much of her life among the mothers and children of the Arab Quarter of the Old City of Jerusalem. She had known peace in Jerusalem, and she could envision it again.

Like her mother, Anna Grace was able to live and work with Arabs, Jews, Englishmen and even Americans. Her happiness centered on her family and on her larger family at the Spafford Center. Hundreds there continue to bless her name. Those of us who were fortunate enough to know her, loved her. The Mother Superior may have been right in telling her she was not cut out to be a nun. But Anna Grace followed her principles and continued to serve God in her own consecrated way, giving of her time, energies, and means unstintingly from the day she walked away from the convent in Oxford until her death in Jerusalem decades later

Anna Grace died on December 2, 1994. Her son, Peter, was with her, and her friend Mary Franji had not left her side for three weeks.

Georgette told me that Anna Grace had been conscious and able to talk until the last few days. Then a peculiar thing happened. During the last week of her life, Anna Grace spoke only Arabic, fluent, beautiful Arabic. Georgette and I laughed together, remembering that Anna Grace had often said she spoke only "kitchen Arabic" because her mother had not felt it fitting for her children to learn it well. At the end, Peter was there as a nun from Ecco Homo, Sister Donna, sang her favorite songs to her and had just finished singing the chant of the Holy Saturday Liturgy, "Come, Lord Jesus," when Anna Grace slipped quietly away from the Jerusalem she loved.

Some who had loved her longest and best were not there, though they would have wanted to be. Among them was Teddy Kollek, the venerable longtime mayor of Jerusalem, who had honored her whenever and wherever he could. They were of an age. They shared a vision of peace in a troubled city and land. She had served with him on a committee for beautifying the city. He told me the city had awarded Anna Grace the prestigious Jerusalem Prize:

> I was elected mayor in December 1965 and the city was divided, but two years later it was reunited. At that time, I went to the American Colony and met Mrs. Vester, her daughter Anna Grace and her son Horatio and daughter-in-law Val Vester. Theirs was one of the institutions that impressed me. They had remained self-sufficient through all that had happened. They could have used many things, but they asked for very little from the city.
>
> Later, Anna Grace's major request from us in the municipality was to do something for the open area behind Herod's Gate. The Jerusalem Foundation did a playground there. We got some money for the playground, and we got some gates for soccer.
>
> We have a title we give, that the city gives, to people over seventy. We give it only to people who are not famous. People who are famous don't need that, they have enough of that. It's called the Patriot of Jerusalem. We give it every year. We gave it to Anna Grace. She came to every occasion whenever we invited her, and I saw her often. From time to time I was able to help.

She was so gentle, and so at peace, and so nice. You hardly find people like that.

We gave her Hebrew medicines and Hebrew help, and here and there a little money. We would have done it anyway, but to do it for her was pure pleasure. She had absolute devotion and a completely decent character. I could feel her gentility and kindness from the first moment.

All those who knew Anna Grace felt these qualities, too. When my daughter visited Jerusalem, Anna Grace wrote me a note and said, "Will you and your daughter have lunch with me?" So we did. What a pleasant afternoon we spent at the American Colony! My daughter remembers the delightful conversation carried on by Anna Grace in her own regal style, an art that is nearly lost in our generation because it takes time. Often we speak of "finding time" to do a thing, as if all the time we lose in aimlessness can somehow be reclaimed. Anna Grace always found time.

Early in 1994, just a few months before Anna Grace died, my husband and I visited the Holy Land with two of our granddaughters. When I called her and told her how much I wanted my granddaughters to meet her, I should have known she would say, "Come for lunch." She was always a gentlewoman, courteous and polite. She treated our granddaughters in the same gracious way she had treated their mother the year before.

The lunch was delicious, but Anna Grace was the best part of the visit. I can still picture that dear little woman, dwarfed by my tall seventeen- and eighteen-year-old granddaughters, every whit the grand dame. Elizabeth, the seventeen-year-old, remembers the visit with joy and fondness: "She knew everything about the land, especially Jerusalem. I loved all the stories she told us. I knew she could tell us much more. She was so dignified and yet friendly and personable."

I will always remember one special afternoon I shared with Anna Grace. As her eyesight dimmed, I read to her by the pool at the American Colony Hotel. It was so peaceful. A little breeze was blowing as we sat under an umbrella and spread the books out on the table before us. We snacked on hummus and sipped cool, fresh lemonade until the sun had set.[8] It was a unique moment, more like the nineteenth century than the twentieth century. Suddenly I was in her world. Later, when we walked up to the Spafford, nearly everyone we passed greeted her. This was her element—these narrow cobbled streets and these struggling Arab folk, especially their babies. She had been heard to say that she didn't like children, but her actions crowded out her words, drowned them out by nearly a lifetime of service to the babies and children of Jerusalem.

It was not easy for Anna Grace to accept compliments. Usually she demurred, shrugging off the sweetness of approbation, disallowing that she deserved any of it. But she did. How many children and adults in the streets of Jerusalem and throughout the world have her to thank for their health, their education, their launching into a vocation? One of the doctors at the Spafford Center had been brought there himself as a sick child. Thus the circle closes and a debt is paid.

With Anna Grace, another cycle of giving also comes full circle. It began with a grandmother after whom Anna Grace was named and with whom she felt a special kinship. Like a stone dropped into a pond, the ripples of peace continue.

Notes

1. When Anna Grace Lind was invited to lecture about her grandparents Horatio and Anna Spafford, she began by quoting NIV Ezekiel 47: 22–23: "You are to allot [this land] as an inheritance for yourselves and for the aliens who have settled among you and who have children. You are to consider them as native-born Israelites; along with you they are to be allotted an inheritance among the tribes of Israel. In whatever tribe the alien settles, there you are to give him his inheritance, declares the Sovereign Lord."
2. *Spafford Children's Center Association Quarterly*, Winter 1992.
3. *Levantine* means a native of the Levant, a name for the countries on the Mediterranean Sea.
4. By pure serendipity I audiotaped a short interview with Peter at the Spafford Center on the morning of March 25, 1993, while he and Georgette were visiting

Anna Grace in Jerusalem. I happened to be at the Spafford Center that day to interview Mary Franji.

5. The heavy snows of 1992 caused severe problems for the municipality. We had five snowstorms, with up to a meter of snow in some places. The snow stayed on the ground for days, causing electrical failures, road-clearing problems and the loss of thousands of trees, which cracked under the unaccustomed weight or simply fell over, exposing shallow roots. Each storm paralyzed the city. Military tanks with dirt-moving blades were finally used to clear the roads.

6. Bertha Spafford Vester, *Our Jerusalem* (Jerusalem: Ariel Publishing House, 1988), 362–63.

7. Everyone in Israel was instructed to outfit a "sealed room" as a defense against Iraqi rockets with chemical warheads. It was a room sealed against poison gases seeping in and was outfitted with food, sanitary facilities and a TV or radio. It was a kind of safe cave in which to wait out a chemical attack.

8. Hummus is a Middle Eastern delicacy, a paste made of chickpeas, tahini, lemon juice, olive oil and a few spices, eaten by dipping pita bread into it. One feels timeless eating it, because something like it has probably been around for millennia.

4. HIND HUSSEINI

You see why I am putting on a shawl. The other day I fell down the staircase because I have a refugee cat. I started to feed her and be very nice to her, and she started to be very nice to me. As I was going down the staircase she screamed, so I didn't know where to put my feet and I fell down three steps and I landed on all fours like the way to pray. I got up to feel if my limbs were OK, and I feel that my hands and my feet are OK. Then at night I started to think that my shoulder is hurting me. I forgot that I fell down, so now I must keep it warm.

Set Hind Husseini

"I forgot that I fell down." That is how Hind Husseini, a pale, sprightly, seventy-seven-year-old Palestinian, took leave of me after our first animated encounter. Such a characteristic statement—forgetting herself had been her lifelong habit. And "I have a refugee cat" was a typical explanation of her concern for the homeless, the helpless. As for ending up on the floor in the Muslim position for prayer—this too was typical of this Muslim woman's life.

I met Hind not through my research into the American Colony in Jerusalem, though I later discovered that Hind had in fact known Bertha Spafford Vester quite well, but through my friend Ulwiya Husseini. Ulwiya had called me excitedly that morning to see if I could come right over to meet her cousin Hind, who was visiting at Ulwiya's home only a few minutes away. Ulwiya had repeatedly urged me to get to know her, so I grabbed my camera and tape recorder and hurried over.

All I knew of Hind Husseini was that she ran a school for Arab orphans and displaced girls in Jerusalem. Only moments into our conversation I discovered that Hind had grown up as a part of the American Colony family. Her home and the school she operated were joined by a gate to the American Colony Hotel. The Husseini family, one of the best-known Arab families in Jerusalem, had property in Sheik Jarrah, a quarter just north of the Old City where they had lived for centuries. Part of their property had been leased and later sold to the American Colony.

Hind described the circumstances of her birth in 1916:

I was born in Jerusalem, in the same house I'm living in. My mother used to come and give birth to us in her father's house. In the same room we're all born, only my eldest brother was born in Istanbul. They found it was much easier for my mother to come here.

I returned to Istanbul as a baby but came back to live in Jerusalem when I was two years old. My father was a lawyer, a judge or something. When he died, we returned to Jerusalem to live.

Hind with her father and brothers

Hind was two years old when her father, Taher Shukri Husseini, died of the plague. She had no memory of him. Her grandfather, Shukri Husseini, served as the acting minister of education in Istanbul. His picture hangs in her sitting room. All of these events took place when the Ottoman Empire was waning. The Turks still occupied and ruled Jerusalem, but the government was in disarray. Perhaps Shukri Husseini's appointment in Istanbul had been an attempt to consolidate what was a disintegrating empire.

Hind was the youngest of six children. She and her five older brothers were reared with four boy cousins who had also lost their father:

Hind with her mother and brothers

We were very happy. We didn't feel at all that we are without fathers. We were very happy all day, playing, and we have nearby this American Colony, Mrs. Vester and Mrs. Whiting and their children, and we play all together. So my best memories, my playing, is something ordinary.

[But my best memory is of] Christmas at the American Colony. Mrs. Vester prepared a very nice Christmas party for all the children of the quarter.

We were sitting, waiting for Father Christmas to enter with his big, big, big basket to give us the presents. I remember the beautiful dolls, once such a big doll they gave me. They were giving very nice Christmas gifts, and sweets. They were packed nicely in red paper. We would eat the Christmas cakes, and then go home.

She is like an auntie to me, Bertha Vester.

We had good times. Easter was very exciting, too . . . coloring the eggs was a happy memory.

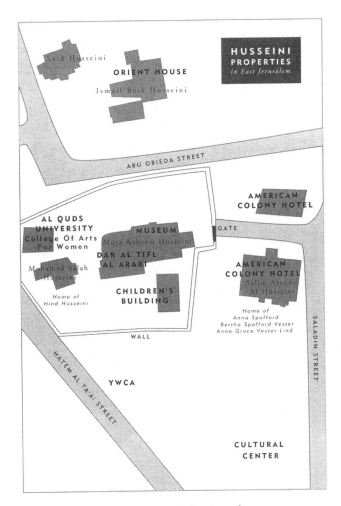

Husseini properties in East Jerusalem

It was Bertha Spafford Vester who included this little Muslim girl in these Christian celebrations.

Hind described the neighborhood in detail and how the three Husseini houses were situated in relationship to the others. They all still stand today. The main building of the American Colony, which had been a pasha's palace, was the main Husseini house.[1] Next to it was her mother's grandfather's house. Nearby was her mother's father's house, the house where Hind lived when I spoke with her—"the grand-grand-daughter's house," she called it.

She spoke of her education:

To start with, I went to the government school, where we were all supposed to go to learn the language and the religion. Then we used to enroll in other schools and I continued with my education in the Jerusalem Girls' College until I finished.

It was the time of the British Mandate. I was two years old when I came. The Mandate lasted from 1918 up until 1948 when I started my work.

Hind's early life was spent in Jerusalem under the British Mandate. Her family had known the occupation of the Turks and then the British, and now she experienced the new state of Israel and Jewish rule.

After she finished her studies at the Jerusalem Girls' College, she was invited to teach in a school near the mosque (the Dome of the Rock), called the Muslim Girls' School. This was the same school that Ismail Bey, the Turkish Minister of Education—and Hind's uncle—had established in 1896 with eighteen-year-old Bertha Spafford and her governess, Miss Brooke, as headmistresses. Whenever Hind spoke of the school, there was a light in her eyes: "It's a beautiful school." She explained that every window had a view of the mosque.

She taught English and Arabic and planned to go to England for further education, but the Arab Rebellion in 1937 interfered:

I meant to go to England and I even had a scholarship, but I couldn't. My mother said, "No, it's wartime, you don't go!" In 1936 we started the six-month strike [an Intifada that became the model for later ones in 1987 and 2000]. By the time it became 1937 and 1938 I was still teaching and waiting. The preparation for war was all on the go.

I continued teaching, but I started to feel that teaching without knowing the children properly is no work. So I shifted to social work. I was very much interested in social work, and we formed a group. We were a group of women who decided to form several societies all over Palestine so that women could start to move more. There were already societies, but we decided to organize them.

Hind traveled, sometimes once a week, through most of the towns and villages in Palestine from Safed in the north to Beersheba in the south. They were working on setting up schools for their children.

We tried to make them interested in kindergartens, you see, and later nurseries. We were fighting illiteracy. So there began to be centers all over for kindergarten, fighting illiteracy and teaching dress-making. Then we started to jump to schools, but unfortunately there was turmoil in the country.[2]

She continued her social work, and though difficult, it was flourishing. In 1945 she and her colleagues started publishing a leaflet.

One woman was responsible for gathering the news. She was traveling very often with me, and we published a leaflet about our work and about what each society was doing. We used to give it to the societies and make them interested with pictures and good articles. It was working beautifully until 1948. Then it was all-out war [the Israeli War of Independence], and all the societies with whom I worked in Jerusalem—we were the main center—they left.

I screamed at them. I said to them, "Now is the time for us to work!" Plenty of them had to leave with their families, you see, it's not their will. And for a time Jerusalem had very few Arab women and men able to work here, the ones who had lived in the Old City. I was not able to stay in our house here in this quarter [Sheik Jarrah, just north of the Old City outside the walls]. It was very dangerous because shooting was coming from Hebrew University [Mt. Scopus] and from the other sides. So we used to be very careful how to move.

Arab, Jewish and Christian women each took war in their stride. The media of today, showing us images of the terrible and bloody, has painted only a partial picture. In war-torn countries everywhere, women grapple with the concerns of daily life, which take them out of their barely safe homes and into the streets. There they search for food or medicine or wandering children gathering up guns and grenades. Living on the edge of war does not change a family's lifestyle entirely. It alters it, to be sure, but the women of Jerusalem have been forced to find alternative ways of doing their work.[3]

When I asked Hind if she left the city, she exclaimed:

No, no, I stayed. I was obstinate. I said to my beloved friend who was publishing the leaflet, "Look here, I am not afraid of death. If a bullet comes and hits me, I don't mind. But I am not ready to leave lame children who are not able to walk. I cannot walk away from them."

My friend was very well educated, more trained because she had been to England for one year. She refused to stay. She said to me, "And you want to work? Go ahead. I'm going to Jericho."

So I had a nursery in the Old City for working mothers where they could put their children and go to work. It was only two rooms, but enough.

We had twelve beds in one room, and in the second room small tables and chairs. When the bullets started to come on Jerusalem, the nursery was empty, so the nurse who was employed there closed it. The helpers who had worked in the nursery had fled to Jericho. Jerusalem started to be filled with refugees from all the surrounding villages. And then they would run to Jericho and from Jericho to Amman, then to Damascus.

Many of the refugees returned gradually. Others settled in the places to which they had fled, especially those who had gone to Amman. Even today, as peace is discussed behind closed doors, one item on the agenda is the return of Palestinians who escaped in 1948 and in other wars since and have not returned. Hind remembers:

But those who were in Jericho came back. In summer, my dear, they couldn't stay. [The heat in Jericho in summer is legendary.] Luckily, they came back. They were coming and going. I can't say all of them came back or all of them stayed out. No, they were going and coming. Jerusalem is dear to everybody.

Many of the old houses collapsed. There was nothing but rubble until they were rebuilt. Most of the houses were disturbed. Maybe not every house, but most of them were disturbed.

The scene is a familiar one in many parts of Jerusalem. Some areas have been cleared and new Israeli buildings constructed. But there are still neighborhoods where one can find collapsed houses and rubble.

Hind speaks of the refugees who poured into the narrow streets of the Old City, its pockmarked buildings disfigured by bullets, groups of children chasing around corners and up narrow alleys:

One day when refugees were pouring into the Old City, they were stationing them in the schools, because there were no other places. The acting mayor of Jerusalem, Anwar El Hatib, called some men and women for a meeting. He was a very good man, a very good man. He was, I think, the only one who could have called us together. He called me also. At that time I didn't know him but it seems that he got my name.

So I went. It was so difficult to jump and enter the Herod's Gate at that time from the Notre Dame de France. They were shooting. We went to the meeting.

On my way to the meeting, passing by the Holy Sepulchre, I saw a strange picture—several little children standing there. They were from two up to eleven years, maybe, or twelve years. I couldn't see them without asking, "What are you doing here? Don't you see bullets are coming? Go home."

I was in a hurry; I wanted to arrive on time to the meeting. I walked maybe two steps, and then I came back. "Why are you standing? Go home, I tell you!"

Then this "elderly lady," eleven years or twelve, I don't know, said, "We are the Deir Yassin children. We are the remnants. We were collected by the Jews, and they brought us through the streets of Jewish Jerusalem [West Jerusalem], and then they put us at Damascus Gate [entrance to the Arab Quarter of the Old City] and they said, 'Go to your people, and they'll look after you.' And here we are."

I became dizzy. I went to the meeting. I put up my hand. I said to them, "Excuse me, but before you start with the agenda, I want to tell you before there is no time." I told them of the children.

So Anwar El Hatib said, "I'm sorry, Miss Husseini, but we are going to discuss the problem as a whole. We have so many refugees, we don't know how to deal with them all." I said to them, "All right, I have an idea," because I had these two rooms as I have told you. I said to them, "You continue with your meeting, but I want to go and see what I can do with the children."[4]

So off went Hind to arrange to open and furnish her two rooms to house the children. She began collecting carpets, blankets and people.

These two rooms were not far from the meeting place. The meeting place was near Damascus Gate, and these two rooms were in the hostel for the German Lutheran Church nearby. My two rooms were down in the basement, and in front of it is a bit of courtyard. When I arrived they were closed, but I knew the house of the nurse and she could help me open it. She was living near the American baby home [the Spafford Children's Home] in the Old City.

I went to the nurse. Her name was Hana El Kharshay. I said to her, "Hana, I want to reopen the nursery, because what I have been seeing. Are you ready to come and work, or shall I see somebody else?" She said, "No, of course I work. I'm not better than you." So, I took her.

We opened the place. We tried to furnish it with these reddish Bedouin carpets, the hand-weaving kind. They were very cheap at that time—five dinars for every carpet, it was. We bought five of them.

These women were trained in crisis. It was their native element. They were not put off by the enormous needs of these homeless children. They had seen the mayor and sensed the time lag that would follow the meeting and any decisions made there. So they just did what needed to be done, with little or no time lag at all.

We said it is now warm. We can manage with the few blankets we have for the whole nursery. And the next day, I went collecting. At the social worker department, I collected a young man who was called Amin Tamini. He said to me, "If you like, I can come with you." Of course I like! Come! And we started collecting children. We collected in that first day and the second day, within that week, around fifty-five children, as far as I remember. People started screaming, "You have so much money. Go and feed those who are hungry."

Those who have never lived on the tightrope of war cannot know what juggling takes place, especially among those who are balancing along the same rope. Imagine having to defend yourself for using what little money you had to save children! But adults get hungry, too, and survival becomes paramount in their minds. If someone else seems to have more, then the idea of fairness urges them to ask for their share. Natural inhibitions lapse. Survival of the fittest seems logical and necessary. But where does that leave the children? In this case, with Hind, who would fend for them:

I said to those who screamed at me, "I don't have much money. I have a little bit of money." I had at that time in my pocket 138 or 148 [dinars, or Palestinian pounds, as they called it]. "And I'm going to live with the children as long as we can, as long as

the money lasts, and then everybody goes home." But unfortu-
nately, many other incidents took place, and here we are.

Not everyone yelled at her, begging for help for themselves. There
were also those who came to Hind to offer their help.

The headmistress of the Ma'muniya School, which is now near
us, was Basima Faris. She came running to me. She said, "Do
you like me to come and help you?" I said, "Please, come."

For a time it was enough, but soon they needed more help.
Imagine feeding fifty to sixty children each day. Even if the meals
were scanty, the never-ending need would far outlast less than two
hundred dinars.

We used to go together to the Old City shopping centers and say
to the merchants, "Come, see and give." That's how it started. It's
a long story. That's how it grew. Then one day, we needed more.
And we said, let us go and see this acting mayor of Jerusalem. We
went. He was stationed in the Alkoff Building near the mosque.

We went together, Miss Faris and myself. There were so
many people, but the doorkeeper knew us from our work.

When we enter, we asked, "Is he busy?" They said, "He is
meeting . . ." but then he opened the door for us. We found him
standing up and speaking.

I never forget that day. Me and Basima listening, and the
Mayor was speaking and did not notice us. He was telling them,
"Look here! If you want me to give you a business license, you
send a sack of potatoes to Hind Husseini at Dar Tefl." They said
to him, "Where do I find this place, this Dar Tefl?" He said to
them, in this and this place, in these two basement rooms . . . You
send rice, you send sugar, or whatever. . . ."

Before we even asked . . . then he looked at us like this [and
she made a wonderful face expressing surprise!] as he saw us
standing at the door, and he said, "What can I do for you?" I said

to him, "Don't ask, what we want is already fulfilled. Thank you very much, and also your merchants." And we went.[5]

There they stood, listening to their shopping list being enumerated before they had even submitted it. It was like a prayer being answered even before you speak the word. In the Old Testament, Isaiah 62:24 describes the process: "Before they call, I will answer; and while they are yet speaking, I will hear."

Later Hind moved into the Old City to be closer to the children in her two rooms. The war was still lumbering along, gunfire a commonplace in the city.

It was very difficult for me to go every day and cross the Herod's Gate so I took a room in Vendicion, in the convent, in the Old City. The Vendicion is pretty. It is two buildings. If you come from Stephen's Gate and go up, the first thing you meet is a convent for mothers, and then comes the Vendicion, two huge buildings, connected with an arch, just after St. Ann's.

There was a very famous school in it. My mother was one of their students, and my auntie. I had been to that school for one year. So I went to them, and they gave me a very nice room. I moved some of my easy chairs that I could sit, because there in the convents they give you only ordinary chairs. I asked them if they minded if I could bring my own chairs and they said, "No, of course, bring what you like."

So, every day, I used to go in the morning to my children and respond to their wishes and see what we could do, and every teacher in the neighborhood came to help.

She was around thirty-one when these orphans became her children. I was touched when she said, "And then I went to my children." I asked her if she had ever thought about marriage for herself. Her reply was quick and enthusiastic, full of energy, though it came from that frail frame: "No, no, no, how can I even think of marriage? I had my children. I was very busy."

The course of the war eventually made it necessary to leave the two rooms for a time.

One day I went to the children, I went alone and I went as usual from the Vendicion to the children up there. I found them sitting again—never forget that sight—making a circle, the little ones in the middle, and sitting and crying, becoming hysteric.

"Why do you make like this? What is the matter with you?" I asked. They said, "We are very much afraid. At night we hear the shooting, and the shooting is coming near us." Really, they were fighting to try to open the gates of the Old City. The Old City gates were very good; they saved the Old City.

So I said to them, "Don't worry. Now I go and fetch my things and come and sleep with you."

I went to Vendicion and was crying, but I started quickly packing some things to take with me. I took a small bag and I was going down. Luckily, the Superior Mother, met me and asked, "Where are you going, Hind?" I said to her, "I am going to my children. So, so, and so happened, and I can't leave them to sleep alone, I want to go and sleep with them." She said, "No, you don't go and sleep with them."

She was very kind, really. She was Spanish, a soft and nice woman. Mere [Mother] Goglade was her name. I never forget her. She said to me, "Come with me, I go around with you and you pick the place you like and bring the children to it."

Her eyes lit up as she described the spot she and the Mother Superior chose that morning:

There are staircases that you can even go up to Mrs. Vester's play-ground. From there you can reach the place quickly. On that staircase there was a door at the side called City Marianne. It's a courtyard and several rooms surrounding it. I said to her, "This would be good for us." She said, "Yes, we'll have it. Go and bring your children." I quickly left my bag, and they prepared and emptied the rooms. And of course, in the meantime, we started to have some mattresses, some covers, some this and that, and everything was dear [costly] to us.

So I went there, I said to them, "Yelleh ["hurry"], children, we are going to go to a very nice place where I am living." And you should see how we were passing though the Old City streets and ruins, some of the children carrying things, and the very little ones each wanted to hold my hand. I cannot hold them all; I was with a pleated, gathered skirt. I said to them, "Yes, you have my skirt."

At that time there were around fifty-five. We couldn't take more than fifty-five to sixty, not more than that. As we passed the Old City streets, people were sometimes laughing, sometimes crying; same with us, 'til we arrived at the Vendicion and there we settled. We continued there for forty-five days exactly. It was very nice, really.

The details came rushing back:

The nuns were helping us. They did many things and we do all the rest of the work. I was going sometimes to see about their food and for this and that, sometimes helping in other places as well.

The Austrian hostel was turned into a hospital. I helped nursing the wounded people. There were plenty of wounded people without nurses. So we used to go and help. We cleaned, rolled bandages, sat beside the wounded people to feed them, to speak with them, and so on.[6]

When Hind saw what needed to be done, she simply did it. Had she watched Bertha Spafford Vester's similar response to the wars and crises she had faced? Perhaps sparks from Bertha lit the flame in Hind, which had not dimmed in her seventy-ninth year.

The little girl who had loved Christmas in the American Colony cared for an impoverished group of orphaned children, just as she

had been cared for and loved. Only these children did not lack a
mother. She became their mother, as she took up as many hands as
she could, while others clung to her ample gathered skirt, and led
them to safety. It was to be her life's work.

That was really how her school began. She continued caring for
the children until the 1948 war ended, with new boundaries and a
new government. Now Hind learned to work with Israelis to find
support for her enterprise.

How did she finally acquire the houses of her Husseini ancestors?
How did she come to reclaim the land of her own childhood? As she
told the story, her joy was palpable.

> When things settled a little bit, we went back to our two rooms in
> the Old City. In time we grabbed some other rooms. And then
> before the end of 1948, the ceasefire took place and I went quick-
> ly, repaired our house [the one next door to the American Colony
> Hotel]—it was damaged. Musa Alami helped us with some money
> to repair it. Five hundred dinars, I think, or a thousand, I don't
> remember. We repaired the whole house, my grandfather's house.[7]

That was the beginning. Later she would manage to reclaim the
land she had played on as a child. In fact, her getting it depended in
large part on her childhood playmates, her cousins.

> So we started to settle there, in the house where I am now.
> Downstairs, we made two rooms into a nursery, and the rest of
> the house for the older children upstairs with me, and we started
> having more children and more and more and more, and we came
> to what we are. Then we grabbed the house of my mother's
> grandfather and made classrooms downstairs and up. We needed
> it as the dormitories.
>   We pulled down the stables—you know the old people used
> to have stables for their horses for their carriages. These stables
> were not good. We pulled them, and we erected the school where
> it is now. It was the donation of the Arab people. They made us

the basement where we have our dining room and some of our
classes. And we are very, very happy.[8]

I asked her when all this had happened, because it seemed almost
instant as she told it. "It was in the end of 1948. In September 1948,
I think, we were in this house, as far as I remember, and we've been
here ever since."

I asked Hind what had caused her to stay in Jerusalem when
other people fled.

It seems that God wants me to work [here]. Believe me, when I
stand now and see this school and see the children, I can't believe
that I do all of this thing, I am amazed. I was always feeling to
go ahead, rolling on. At first, I was alone and then people start-
ed coming and helping.

This was, of course, an understatement. She took the lead over
and over again to find the funds and goods to go on. But it did, indeed,
sound like she had her angels who were at the crossroads with just the
help she required. She was never shy. She let others know what she
was seeking. The miracle, perhaps, was that these others had the
resources to supply her and decided to do it. Yet, after knowing her
even briefly, I can understand their willingness to help Hind.

One day, before Aramco [a prosperous Saudi oil company] came
to help us, we had badly broken walls, only stacks of stones, you
know, we didn't have these proper walls around us and the land
was not even, it was built like steps, terraces, and between every
step and the other were also walls. Always I was worried, the
children playing with the stones; that they might take one stone
here and one there and the whole wall might fall and injure the
children.

The solution to this problem involved an improbable, fascinating
tale of making the sacred pilgrimage to Mecca called "The Haj."[9]

In 1949 I went with my mother to Saudi Arabia. She wanted to fulfil her pilgrimage [to Mecca]. So I went with her, and it was so difficult. It was very primitive there, really awful. While we were there, in the most difficult stage, I said, "God, all these people are coming to worship you, and I come, too, but I promise if you only will help me to build our broken walls, I'm ready to come again and worship even if I'm going to die here." Believe me, believe me, this happened.

I went back. And one day they said to me, "An American man is downstairs, he cannot go the staircase, and he would like to see you." I went down to see this American man. It was Colonel Eddie. He was once the director of the American University in Cairo. My eldest brother and one of my uncles were his students. Ulwiya's husband was one of his colleagues. [Ulwiya beamed, "He was a very good friend of ours."]

He said to me, "Hind, I knew you as a child," and I said to him, "Yes?" I didn't remember him really, but he was familiar. I sat with him. We asked for a coffee, they brought us, and he said to me, "I was very much interested. I saw these children while in the American Colony [just across the wall] and I asked, 'What is there?' and they told me what you are doing, so I came to see you."

We spoke and spoke, and he asked me about certain things. "What can we do for you?" he said.

"I don't know, we need first of all to build these walls."

He said to me, "Yes, and you need a school." So he was the one who went to Aramco and spoke to them about me and my work and they came and made me the school in place of the rubbish places we had and he built me the walls and I couldn't believe it. God answered. This is one thing that happened that I can never forget.

She clapped her hands in delight as she remembered. What was there to say after this story? Prayers are answered. Prayers from Mecca, from Calcutta, from Jerusalem, it is the same. But one doesn't

sit in a corner with outstretched hand waiting for such answers—not
if one is Hind Husseini. On the contrary, all antennae are constantly
out. Then prayers are regularly asked and answered.

Help came from other sources as well, and in a variety of ways.

*Then after that, one day I was in the room I am living in now,
and my mother was sitting on the balcony while I was sitting on
a cushion by the door and reading a magazine. In this magazine
they put a report about the prince in Kuwait who started the
schooling there. He used to be called Sheik Amaderas.*

*The magazine spoke a lot about him and they showed pic-
tures that he is interested in schooling and in helping and in this
and that. I wrote a letter by hand, not typed, and I sent it to him.
I said to him that I read about you and so and so. Within fifteen
days I received a check for five hundred sterling and I liked that
very much. I was badly in need of money. Those five hundred
were very valuable to me. I was very happy.*

*After a few months a group from Kuwait came to employ
teachers for Kuwait. They used to come and take teachers. I read
about them in the newspaper. I knew one of them, Mr. Darwish
McDaddi. He was one of the workers who did a lot for Kuwait
concerning education. I rang him up. He was in the El Zahara
Hotel, which was very new at the time and very famous.*

The El Zahara Hotel still stands and is well known in the
Palestinian community. It is only a short distance from Hind's compound, Dar Tefl.

*I said to him, "Mr. McDaddi, probably you remember me. I am
Hind Husseini, and your sheik has contributed five hundred sterling for us. I would like you to come and see the place and go
back and tell him where his money is." He said to me, "Wait,
wait, wait a minute." They had with them their chief, Nabil
Abdil Hussein. So he called the secretary, Mr. Edwin, I think, and*

he said, "We can come to you only now. Instead of having our cof-
fee and rest we will come and see you."

Resting in the afternoon is a Middle Eastern custom. One would
never call on a friend between the hours of one and four, which are
the hottest time of the day. Walking during this same period is most
fatiguing and avoided strenuously by Jerusalemites.

They came, and they walked around and saw. Then the man,
Nabil Abdil Hussein, said to me, "What are you doing here, Miss
Husseini?"
  I said to him, "What you have seen."
  "Why are you staying here?" he asked. I said to him, "Where
to go and leave my children?" He said, "Come to us, and we can
help you a lot."
  I said to him, "I don't come like this. I don't know how to
come like this." He said, "No, we'll extend an invitation." I
answered him quickly, "But I don't like to take from governments.
I like always to have from people to people. Excuse me, but if I
take from a government then I have to follow their policy." He
said, "All right, we will arrange so that you can visit our schools,
meet the children, the teachers, and speak to them and show
them your leaflets."
  So I said to myself, "Oh, this is very good."

She smiled and laughed softly as she spoke of her joy in being
invited to visit Kuwait. In 1958, Hind visited kindergarten and primary schools in Kuwait.

They were having so many schools just starting newly and fur-
nished beautifully with furniture from London, which cost them
so much. The schools were properly built and very nice. Pillars
and luxury.

How did Hind feel when she saw the contrast between her simple
school and the luxurious schools of Kuwait? It made little difference

to her. She returned to telling me about the struggles of raising children and raising funds in Jerusalem. She loved what she did, and she loved telling me about it. Though she didn't covet the wealth she had seen in Kuwait, she felt it was important to reclaim her family's land.

I want to tell you something very important. I wanted to buy the rest of the compound, my mother's grandfather's house, so I wrote my four boy cousins, who all owned shares of the compound and who were also without a father and playing with us as children.

One day I had the idea, I wrote each one. I said to them, "Ask your brother and answer me." Salim was his name. I said to him, "Salim, we have spent a lovely time as children. We didn't feel that we were orphans playing in these playgrounds and living in these beautiful houses. What about making our children as happy as we were as orphans?"

All three quickly answered and said you do what you like and buy our shares and pay what you can. So I started buying shares. They are not the only owners, I had other cousins, and so I started to buy and pay according to what I had. At the end of every year if I had some dinars, I would buy. I started buying in 1958 and I have finished only in 1975, buying shares, and now own the whole compound. There were so many, the grand-grand cousins of my mother and then my uncles and their children. They all helped, and so it worked.

As our time together grew short, I became eager to hear about Hind's relationship with Bertha Vester. They were connected by their desire to help children. They were also neighbors, because the American Colony and Hind's school had only one of those prayed-for walls separating them—a well-built, strong wall with a gate!

Mrs. Vester used to have a baby home and when her babies would grow up, she used to hand them to me and when I used to have babies who were in need of care before they entered the school, I used to give them to her. We had a very good connection together.

What did Bertha look like?

She was very handsome. She was beautiful, with a very graceful body. A smiling face, always. Beautiful features. She was the most beautiful person, maybe, in Jerusalem. She had a style of her own. She was a real lady, and Mr. Vester, her husband was also a nice man. He was a German.

Hind spoke of her with gentleness, a softness, such as one might use in describing a beloved sovereign or princess. After this description of her physical attributes, I asked her if she was likeable. I had learned that one can be beautiful and talented and envied by contemporaries— or cordially disliked. Others I had asked about Bertha had admired her as a strong, powerful woman but had not always liked her.

I really liked her. She was a wonderful woman. I was impressed by her but also liked her. She was very friendly with everybody. She was a Christian. She was keeping Christmas.

As she spoke of Bertha's Christianity, I wondered how religious this little Muslim woman was. I asked her if she prayed, because praying five times a day is the practice that usually distinguishes a devout Muslim. "Yes, I pray, at least once a day. Not five times but once in the morning. If I don't pray in the morning, I feel I cannot work." Her answer spoke to me at the deepest levels of my own religious practice, and I said, "Me, too. *Anna kaman.*" She laughed at my Arabic.

As far as I remember I never missed my morning prayer. My mother used to pray and fast. My mother was a very nice woman. Not less than Mrs. Vester, but she was very busy with us all the time.

Her answer, pairing her mother and Mrs. Vester in this way, caused me to surmise that her busy mother's own ministrations to her had been supplemented by Bertha's. Bertha had helped fill the gaps in the childhood of this woman who had described herself as alone but not an orphan at the death of her father.

I suggested that it was easy to see that her mother had been a nice woman because one could see some of her mother in her—and some of Mrs. Vester, too. "No," she insisted, "my mother was much more beautiful. I'm not." [See the photo of her lovely mother with her children on page 42.]

I cried out silently, "Oh, yes you are! If only you could see yourself." The beauty of her life shone from her deeply lined face. She had earned this beauty by hundreds of separate acts of love, which had been so natural to her that she would never have been able to identify or own them.

As she prepared to leave, she pulled her shawl over her shoulder. I hated to see her go but I knew she had a pressing agenda beyond the walls of this gracious house. Though she enjoyed recounting her remarkable life, its miracles, its drama, still, there was more to be done, and she must be about doing it. I knew this window of time was a gift. Yet, I wanted to keep her there just as long as I could. But in a moment she was gone.

I stood, not wanting to move away from the aura she had left. I learned later from others that she was always addressed as Set Hind, "Lady Hind." I understood that intuitively on that first wonderful day with her.

Several times after that we visited on the phone. We spoke as old friends, as though we had known each other for decades. We spoke of meeting again, but I was conscious of her weakened condition during chemotherapy. She would say, "Perhaps I shall not be so tired tomorrow. Come to me then?" But the tomorrows lengthened, and we never saw each other face to face again.

Set Hind Husseini died in November 1994. Her last strenuous encounter was not with a government official or potential donor but with cancer, a thing that seemed unthinkable on that lovely spring morning when we met. How indestructible she seemed as she walked away, rather briskly, to continue her work.

My faith whispers that she is bustling about in her corner of heaven, doing the kind of good that came so naturally to her. The idea of immortality is bolstered in me as I think of Set Hind. I cannot imagine her silent, lacking the power she had honed to perfection to bring peace, love, and joy wherever she was. I picture her, still completely unconscious of herself, reaching, lifting, crying out to those around her, "*Yelleh* ("hurry"), we must be about our business. There is much to be done."

Notes

1. *Pasha* was a title conferred by the sultan of the Ottoman Empire to designate a man of high rank or office, such as a mayor of a city.
2. The turmoil was caused by the British Mandate coming to an end. Jewish Zionists were pushing for nation status, and with the recent liberation of the Nazi death camps, the world's guilt over the millions of Jewish deaths contributed to the formation of a Jewish homeland.
3. Living in Jerusalem from 1987 to 1993, I experienced daily concerns that had to be fitted in around the Intifada. Our first year, though there was no Intifada, there were occasional bombings and shootings—random acts of terror. I remember the first time I found Ben Yehuda Street cordoned off because of the possibility of a bomb. I had been rushing there to pick up some photos, which I was most anxious to get. On finding the street blocked off and crowds of people waiting, I at first hurried away a bit frightened, wondering why the others waited. But then, having lived among these intrepid folk for less than a year, I, too, decided to wait. When the sappers (Israeli bomb squads) came to open the street, I rushed to do my errands, which had been delayed only fifteen minutes. As I was returning down the hill with a crowd of other shoppers who had entered the empty street like a bunch of marathon runners, I thought to myself, "Only a few minutes and a few meters separate us from a potential bomb." Terrible bombings on that same street have killed dozens since that time. I do not know of the carnage firsthand; all I know is how the threat of it felt.
4. "That mayor died a month, or maybe forty-five or fifty days ago," she said. I remembered the publicity and the outpouring of love for him at his death. Not only the Palestinians but many Israelis spoke highly of him, and there were articles in the papers about the remarkable good he had done for the city.
5. This mayor may have been Amin Majaj (see chapter 6).
6. Dr. Amin Majaj turned the Austrian hostel into a hospital. It is only a few doors west of the Vendicion.

7. Musa Alamee was active in helping orphan boys at a ranch near Jericho run by the Arab Development Society.

8. At one time the kindergarten had 209 children, in five sections. The elementary school had 360 girls, ages seven through thirteen. Prep 12 classes included computers and a secretary section; there were 455 girls in thirteen sections. Two classes were also taught in housekeeping, sewing, knitting, and so forth, with 81 students. These figures are taken from the Hind Husseini Memorial Booklet published soon after her death and translated for me by Malak Sharaf.

9. The Haj is a pilgrimage to Mecca and the boxlike Kaaba. This ritual requires marching with millions of other white-clad followers of the great prophet Mohammed. I had previously thought that only men were allowed to participate in this highest ritual of Islam.

5. Ulwiya Husseini

My idea and feeling is that since I really believe in a religion, there is always somebody behind me helping me. That's why when I have a problem and anything troubling me, after prayer I am relaxed and I feel that the burden weighs a little bit less. I pray for many things to happen and they happen. This makes me feel like I have somebody with me helping me all the time.

Ulwiya Husseini

The February evening was just perfect for a family party. Jerusalem has long periods of mild weather, and we gathered outside to enjoy the sunset and the coolness that followed. My husband and I were the only strangers and foreigners in the gathering, but we were made to feel like family. As dusk came we migrated into small groups, and in each one the conversation was lively.

Hatem Husseini and his wife, Rabee'a, joined us. They were visiting Jerusalem from the United States, where Hatem was a professor at Shaw University. He had lectured at Duke and other American universities and had lived in the States for almost twenty-five years. This handsome, charming young couple spoke impeccable English.

Hatem's mother and our hostess, Ulwiya Husseini, personified the generous hospitality of the Middle East. We were served wonderful food in quantity and the discourse was animated, centering on the return from the States of her young cousin and surrogate grandson Ghaleb Husseini. For eleven years during his childhood, Ghaleb had grown up next door to Ulwiya, calling her Nana. He had returned home from the States for the summer vacation after his first year of study at Brigham Young University. I had taught at BYU for eleven years before traveling to Jerusalem to teach, so we had much to talk about. We were pleased to hear news from Utah, and Ghaleb was more than happy to report on his exciting first year abroad.

The party was intended to allow Ghaleb and Hatem to greet their large extended family. I enjoyed meeting everyone, but it was our soft-spoken hostess in particular whom I hoped to meet again. She lived in a neighborhood adjoining ours.

Only a few days later, my husband suggested I invite a friend to accompany me to that evening's concert given by the Israeli Philharmonic orchestra. I immediately thought of Ulwiya and phoned her, apologizing for the short notice. She seemed hesitant and asked what the program would be. When I replied that it was to be a concert version of *Aida,* she said she and her recently deceased husband had heard it performed in Egypt and it was one of her favorites. She said she would hurry to be ready in time for us to come for her. The ride in the van with our friends was pleasant and congenial.

Not until we entered the Binyanei Ha'Uma concert hall did it occur to me how difficult this evening might be. It was during the first Intifada, and Jews and Palestinians had marked an invisible line beyond which the other was not to go. There were stringent, unwritten rules about fraternizing with the enemy. If not actually transgressing the rules, Ulwiya had at least stepped onto the line. I realized that she had probably hesitated to accept my invitation because of the implications for herself, a Palestinian, in an auditorium filled with Israelis.

We made our way to our seats just in time for the music to begin and sat side by side, enthralled. During intermission, an Israeli friend on my right invited me to bring my husband to dinner the next weekend. This took only moments, and as I turned to introduce Ulwiya, I found she was already conversing with the Jewish woman on her left. I overheard the woman invite Ulwiya to her home for tea, and when Ulwiya quietly said, "My name is Ulwiya Husseini," the woman quickly and graciously responded, "My husband speaks Arabic. Please come."

Peace is a heart-to-heart matter. I don't know, but I doubt Ulwiya went to her new friend's home. It would have been complicated and dangerous to both hostess and guest for a Palestinian to enter a Jewish neighborhood at that time.

From that evening on, Ulwiya and I spoke on the phone often. She graciously agreed when I asked her if she would tape an interview with me, but she said that her cousin Hind was the one I really should talk to. Because I didn't know Hind Husseini, I avoided the suggestion. We decided on a day and time for Ulwiya to share her own history with me.

On the morning of our appointment, we sat sipping anise seed tea from tiny glass cups banded with gold. Her homemade sweets, which accompanied the drink, melted in my mouth. I could see how this hospitality ritual encouraged conversation and sharing. It was so comfortable there in her sun porch. A luxurious hoya plant, just like my grandmother's, trailed up the wall. Each fragrant, velvet bloom had its own tiny red star and dew drop. I was at home.

Ulwiya began to tell me about herself:

*I was born in Jerusalem, close to Damascus Gate in what we call
Musrara. It is just outside of the Old City wall and not far from
Herod's Gate. We were in a temporary house because we lived in
Damascus at the time. I was delivered by Dr. Kagen, a Jewish
woman doctor whom my uncle, Dr. Kamel Husseini, [who
Ulwiya said was the first Arab medical doctor in Jerusalem] had
helped get started. All the family knew her.*

Because she had not mentioned when she was born, I asked if she
wished to say her birth date. She replied in a way I soon learned was
characteristic of her: "I am old enough to have the courage to say. It
was on March 9, 1920."

So she was a few days less than seventy-three years old on the day
we talked. She seemed youthful, a beautiful, slender woman with
quiet charisma. Her silver hair was cut in a fashionably short style.
Her demeanor was calm, yet her smile, when she was animated, was
contagious. Her manner was subdued, which I assumed was on
account of her husband's death several months earlier.

Ulwiya's maiden name had also been Husseini, so her name had
not changed since her birth. The family had been in Jerusalem for
centuries.

*We are supposed to be the descendants of the Prophet Mohammed
through his daughter, Fatima. Her son was Hussein, and we are
descended from him. They would have come to Jerusalem some-
time after A.D. 670 and the Islamic invasion. The Arabs lived in
Jerusalem before this time, but they were not Muslims.*[1]

This exchange reminded me of speaking to Jews who are Cohens
or Levys and whose genealogy has somehow been preserved through
the ages. It is remarkable, but it is characteristic. They know of their
roots, though they span centuries.

Ulwiya's earliest memories were all pleasant, filled with the joys of
childhood. They were such a contrast to the tumultuous life she came

Ulwiya, standing, with her parents, grandmother,
brothers and sister

to know as an adult. She recalled an experience that demonstrates a
maturing sense of obedience and the security she felt as a child:

> *I was six years old and had just taken my piano lesson. The*
> *teacher left me in the room with instructions to practice and then*
> *went away and forgot me. It didn't matter to me. I just practiced*
> *on and on.*

When her teacher discovered her hours later, she was still playing the piano.

Ulwiya's father, S'aid Husseini, was an electrical engineer. He
studied in Istanbul (now Constantinople) and, Ulwiya said, became
the first electrical engineer in Jerusalem. He worked on telephone
lines between Syria and Palestine, which in reality meant between
Damascus and Jerusalem. He had a title from the Turkish government
that reflected his social and government position. In 1927, at the age
of thirty-nine, he fell into a deep well, which caved in. He lay in the

hospital, bleeding internally, for twenty days before he died. Ulwiya's mother, Fakhreyh, was twenty-seven, and Ulwiya was seven.

Memories of her father were vivid. They had spent many happy hours together.

> *We had lived just outside Jaffa Gate, but Father decided, when the Turks left Jerusalem, to go to his own land in Beit Jibreen near Hebron [by the old Roman church] and farm there, using irrigation. We had a large house, and he enlarged it still more.*
>
> *He bought a car. He sometimes took me to school, first in a buggy and then in the car. He used to stop whenever I wanted to pick flowers for my teachers.*
>
> *He was very kind, a real gentleman. I don't remember his ever shouting. But he always made me drink my milk.*

She had one sister and two brothers. In the tradition of her people it was thought that men should be separate from women. If a woman learned to read and write, she might write to a man, thus defeating the separation between the sexes. Nevertheless, many women of this time, and even earlier, went to school.

Ulwiya remembered that one of her aunts spoke French, but her mother had never been to school. She had taught herself to read, and loved reading books and magazines. She made certain her children had every educational advantage.

> *My mother wasn't illiterate. She learned much of the Koran by heart. She would hold the Koran in her lap and analyze the letters until she had learned to read.*

Ulwiya's first school was the well-known Schmidt's School in East Jerusalem. Students of various ages were taught in each grade. Ulwiya was two years younger than all the rest, yet she excelled in her work. Each day a special carriage took her the few miles to school, and she loved the ride. Later she boarded at Schmidt's when her father settled on his farming land close to Hebron. Her second school was a private elementary school called the Islamic School. Then she attended the Women's Training College in Mea Shearim, the ultra-orthodox Jewish neighborhood that separates East and West Jerusalem. It was an exclusive college that sought out the finest students to receive scholarships. Only sixteen Palestinian girls were admitted each year. Ulwiya received the best scholarship and trained to become a teacher.

After her father died, Ulwiya says, she never had the feeling she was fatherless. She knew how much her mother had loved S'aid and how much each of the children was loved. She often remarked on the closeness of her family and how important it is to have love in a home. She felt that love in her own home, yet secretly she believed she was her father's favorite.

My mother wanted us to know that our father had had a good salary so she would say, "He was offered a golden English pound a day." It was not enough to say thirty English pounds a month. But he never took it. He would not work for the British. She wanted us to know that, too.

Her mother died in 1994. She had been such a positive force in her daughter's life. When she knew she was dying, Ulwiya's mother, Fakhreyh, implored her nephew: "Amin, of course I love you. Please call your son S'aid, after my dear husband, so that seventy years later there will be another S'aid."

He was happy to comply.

Ulwiya explained how she became acquainted with her husband, Ishak. As she spoke of his four brothers—Ibrihim, Dauod, Musa and Mohamed—she told me the family joke that without Mohamed the names could easily be taken for Jewish—Abraham, Isaac, David, Moses. Before she met Ishak Husseini in person, she became acquainted with him through his writings. She admired his scholarship.

Sixteen years older than Ulwiya, Ishak grew up in Jaffa and went to London to get his Ph.D. Ulwiya first met him at his brother's house, which was in her neighborhood.

I remember running to the YMCA to hear his lecture but he was not there due to illness and his cousin read the lecture. I was very disappointed, and I wrote asking for a copy of his paper. I wouldn't have dared to write except that I knew his cousin.

He sent the paper, and their friendship began. She remembers fondly that they went walking because he liked to walk. She described his dark blue eyes and bemoaned that fact that not even one of her children had blue eyes. Soon he asked for her hand, and the marriage was arranged in the Middle Eastern way. The families met, they drank coffee together, and when they agreed, the marriage was arranged. He paid a dowry. They were married in 1940. She was twenty, and he was thirty-six.

At the time she was teaching but had to quit because of a British law that forbade Palestinian women to teach if they were married. She had taught one year but was paid for the next three, even though she had stopped teaching. Interesting bureaucracy!

Ishak and Ulwiya lived in a home she loved in Upper Baka, on the southwest border of Jerusalem.[2] Ulwiya describes the location in the context of the 1948 war:

Our home was like the filling in the middle of a sandwich. There was a Jewish settlement behind us, Jerusalem in front of us. Shells came from both sides over us. One day I was alone in the house with the children. Hatem, age five, was the oldest and held onto my dress as the bombs shrilled overhead. Bishr was three, and Nawar was a year and a half.

I tried to calm the children, though I was so frightened myself. I tried to decide if the walls would fall down any moment—they shook so violently—or whether they would last longer. I took the children to the balcony to watch the columns of smoke. Bishr said, "I wasn't afraid, Mommy, but my heart pounded and my knees shook."

Ishak's office was next to the King David Hotel, which was not a great distance from Baka, but the shelling prevented his returning home. Ulwiya was alone with the children during much of the fighting that went on around them. They received obscene calls with a voice shouting, "We'll kill you," trying to frighten them into moving out, but they stayed.

I felt so helpless, alone with my children and without personal arms of any kind and no protection from any army or government. My thoughts ran to feelings of frustration and, of course, fear. I thought, I'll hold Nawar's hand and Bishr's hand but what of Hatem?

We stayed two months. Then it got worse, much worse. My husband called one day and said, "Get the passports ready, we have to move," and we moved early in the morning on one of those beautiful days in Jerusalem. But it was a bad and sad one in our lives.

We believed that we certainly were coming back. We believed it so much that I did not take anything from the house. Some people left their jewelry and money stashed away in their homes.

That was in March 1948. The family traveled to Aleppo, where her maternal aunts lived. Her husband stayed to finish business in Jerusalem before joining the family.

We rented a house in Aleppo—a large, empty school. It was unfurnished, but we believed it would only be temporary because we intended to return soon to Jerusalem.

I was very tidy in this new place, but Nawar was never happy. Even as a baby of nearly two years, she was used to her own surroundings—her bed, toys and her own room. When this was lost, she too was lost. I remember that she just sat crying all the time. She just sat and looked at the unfamiliar surroundings and cried and sometimes wouldn't stop. She reflected how we all felt. She never stopped crying.

The family remained in Aleppo not just a few days or weeks but one and a half years, living on money they had saved. Then Dr. William Eddy from the American University of Beirut offered Ishak a job teaching Arabic.[3] So they moved to Beirut and remained seven years. During that time Ishak went twice to Canada as a visiting professor.

Ulwiya adored and respected her husband. She focused her attention on his success:

All my life I tried very hard to make my husband feel at ease and to concentrate on his work and his writings because he was such a good writer. I enjoyed what he wrote, so I tried very hard to enable him to produce more. He was alone with his books, his studies, and his writing, and I used to be the only one who looked after the home and the family. Maybe that's why I have this energy.

My judgment of him turned out to be very true. Years after we got married, he won the first prize for the best novel in the whole Arab world. In Jerusalem, in 1986, he was elected to be the first dean of Arabic literature.

In 1955 Ishak accepted a position in the Arabic Department at American University in Cairo, Egypt. At the same time, he was offered a place in the Arab League Institute for Palestinian Studies. Since they were not at all certain they would want to live in Cairo, Ishak spent one year alone there to explore the possibility of moving his family to Egypt while Ulwiya stayed on in Beirut with the children.

Because of our emigration and losing everything, the most important decision was how to earn a new living. That was the decision that was imposed on us. We used to talk about it endlessly. We might have had more children were it not for our unsettled life. How could we bring more children into this situation? We lived in Beirut, Lebanon, while Ishak taught at the American University of Beirut. It was a lovely place to live.

Then it came to him to move over to the American University in Cairo and to another institute, an Arabic institute for graduate students. That was a problem for us to decide. Should we go or not go? It was a big step. We kept talking about it for a long time, and then we decided. . . . I encouraged him to go by himself for the first year and I would stay in Beirut with the little kids. Believe me, it was not easy. I had no telephone at home, no car, with three little children. But I wanted him to go to be sure about himself because he was not entirely happy in Beirut.

In 1956 Ulwiya moved with the children to Cairo. It was not an easy move. Some areas were safe and she could feel comfortable, but there was much poverty and living conditions were poor. It was a huge adjustment.

She started a clinic in Cairo with some other Palestinian women. They did this under the supervision of the Palestinian Red Crescent.[4] Later, they established Al-Quds Hospital.[5]

She also had other projects:

For about ten years I worked teaching embroidery to young refugees. This Palestinian embroidery art had been neglected as a result of the immigration [of Palestinians to Jordan, Syria, Lebanon and Egypt after 1948] and the difficult living conditions in refugee camps. The women were concerned with other matters and didn't have the materials to do the embroidery.

Our job was to restart this old and beautiful tradition. Young girls were taught to practice and they started again. The Egyptian ladies wear black, long gowns and though we started out wearing our beautifully embroidered dresses, we adopted their custom. They used to pull over when they saw us in those embroidered dresses, thinking that we were going to a wedding.

Ulwiya's gracious home in northeast Jerusalem was filled with colorful embroidered pillows, wall hangings, and other pieces that gave her surroundings a bright beauty.

I loved it when we went to the young women's houses and I began teaching them to embroider. We started with small pieces, samples of different traditional patterns. I still have some of the samples I used to teach them. I loved teaching young women this art from their grandmothers. I think it helped them gain an appreciation for their culture. It became a framework for preserving other parts of their culture as well.

This craft had been a comfort to her in time of war:

The war started on Monday morning. I was devastated and began to embroider and this way I took my homeland with me one stitch at a time.

In 1967 Ulwiya and Ishak began construction on a home to retire to in Jerusalem. This time their home would not be in Baka but in the northeast section between East Jerusalem and French Hill. Ulwiya visited Jerusalem in 1967 to see how the building was progressing, leaving behind her husband and children in Cairo.

I came to Jerusalem for only fifteen days to check on our house, which was being built. I called my husband in Cairo when I could see that things were unsettled. I didn't want to lose another house in Jerusalem. I had walked away leaving everything behind once and I didn't want to do it again.

I asked Ishak if I might stay to look after our partly built house—the one in which we are now sitting. He said, "Draw out all our money from the Amman Bank and bring it and come as fast as you can." He was afraid for me and felt we should be together if there was to be fighting again. So I didn't stay the last five days because I felt war in the air—the Jordanian troops had left. I went to Amman and flew out from there just four days before the so-called Six Day War.

I felt I should stay and save our home. We had put all our retirement savings into it. I didn't want to lose this retirement

*home. My husband was a professor, not a rich man. We could
never afford to do this again.*

*I am not a coward. I was in Cairo during three wars, in
1956, 1967 and 1973. In 1956, it was only the second night for
us in our apartment when the war broke out. Our home was a
couple hundred meters away from Al-Maza military airport. The
fragments of the bombs settled in the walls of the house, and
some were in the balcony. We did not flee. Women joined the civil
defense and attended the wounded at the hospitals.*

*Once I had to walk for two miles to get to my sister's home to
check up on her. I had to seek shelter at stores and in buildings
along the way during the air raids. My husband wrote about this
incident in his memoirs, saying, "She is a very courageous woman."*

But because her husband insisted that she return to their home in
Cairo, she barely missed being in yet another war.

Just as the 1967 war began, she told me, one of her male cousins
was standing, unarmed, in the garden at Dar El Tifl (Hind Husseini's
school for orphan girls) when a fully armed Israeli soldier parachut-
ed into the garden. Astonished, the two young men stared at each
other. The Israeli expected to be cut down by the Palestinian, but
when he saw that his enemy had no weapon, he looked over his
shoulder and let the Palestinian go. Such may sometimes be the real-
ities of war. Dehumanization is not always the rule. Yet such stories
as this one are not the kind our media ferret out.

Two years later, in 1969, Ishak began a one-year term as a visiting professor at Smith College, in Northampton, Massachusetts. I was
startled when Ulwiya mentioned these events because during that
same school year, my husband and I also lived in Massachusetts while
he was a visiting professor in Boston. During that year we visited
Smith College, but our paths were not yet to cross with the
Husseinis'.

In 1970 Ishak and his family returned to Egypt. Four years later,
after twenty-two years in exile, they finally received permission to
return to Jerusalem. It felt to Ulwiya like a miracle, or at least an
answer to prayer that had been a long time coming.

Ulwiya's family

Not long after they were settled in their new home in northeast Jerusalem, they welcomed into the adjoining apartment their newly married relatives, Adnan and Rafif Husseini. Adnan's father is Ulwiya's cousin. For eleven years they were more than neighbors. The children of Adnan and Rafif called their neighbor Nana Ulwiya. She helped young Ghaleb with his English homework. She enlisted the help of all the children in her beloved garden, weeding among the roses and the sweet-smelling trellises of wazzal, a fragrant plant that is a favorite of hers. She always had treats for them in exchange for the work, but Ghaleb remembers that he would have done it just to experience her joy in the beauty they helped her to maintain. She became another grandmother to the children and a second mother to Rafif.

Ghaleb exclaimed, "My mother adored Nana Ulwiya, and she has become very much like her." He remembers:

I was nine and a half when we moved away. Nana Ulwiya and Ishak's family were always thought of as a wonderful family, beloved by the rest of the Husseinis. They were such a nice cou-

ple, so lighthearted together. You could feel their love for each other. She was an inspiration to him.

When I showed Ghaleb a photograph of Ishak and Ulwiya surrounded by their family, he immediately named each one. After each identification he unconsciously exclaimed, "Oh, I love him" or "Oh, I love her." It was a tender testimonial.

Shortly after Ulwiya and her family returned to Jerusalem, Ishak was asked to be president of Al-Quds University and to spearhead efforts to establish this institution of higher learning for the Palestinians. This he did with vigor, until his unexpected death on December 17, 1990, at age eighty-six, after a distinguished career as an educator, writer and university president.

Ulwiya felt his loss deeply. She kept a memorial corner dedicated to him with his photo and other memorabilia. They had shared almost exactly fifty years together. "We lived together for quite a good and long time," she often said. Her focus was on preserving his work, and she gathered materials to have unpublished works published and other items republished. As a Muslim, she believed that the timing of Ishak's death was the will of Allah, but that did not blunt the pain of separation which she obviously felt years later.

One bright spot in her life was the hope that her son Hatem might return to live in Jerusalem. Excitedly, she told me the news that he had been asked to carry out the task his father had earlier accepted—to head Al-Quds University. Soon Hatem would be home in Jerusalem, and her dream would come true. An illness delayed his leaving the States, but finally the day came when he returned. She was overjoyed. All her prospects seemed bright, and she felt blessed.

Hatem returned to Jerusalem to live in 1993 and began his task with energy. On November 11, 1994, he wrote of a proposed medical school:

Every Palestinian should feel proud that a new Palestinian medical college is on its way to being established in Jerusalem. This is a dream that has long been with us. However, the tensions of war and conflict kept us from building essential educational institutions for our people. . . .

In less than six years we will enter the twenty-first century. We must face the challenges with professional and excellent institutions.

Those who tell us to move slowly are wrong. We have to move fast, we have to mobilize all our energies, and we have to act as if we are in a state of emergency. We have wasted enough precious time and resources. The excellent Palestinian doctors have left us for Europe and the United States because we have not built our own medical institutions. . . .

In order to succeed we must unite all our efforts, and cooperate and support each other. . . .

Let us keep the dream alive and let us join hands to build what is best for our Palestinian people.[6]

Brave, wonderful words from a powerful young man who knew he was suffering from terminal cancer. He knew better than anyone what advantages would come to his people with a fine medical school. He died in December 1994.

Ulwiya was crushed. She couldn't believe it. How could this be the will of Allah? She was nearly inconsolable.

I had already returned to live in the States, so I had not known of her mother's death earlier in the year nor of the death of Ulwiya's brother, who had preceded his mother by four months. But I did hear of Hatem's untimely death and called her immediately. I knew her heart must be broken. And it was. She cried out, "I have nothing to live for now. He was my great hope. What can I do? There is no reason for me to keep living."

I found myself searching for words of comfort, reasons for her to continue living. I reminded her of her faith in Allah's will, but this seemed a hollow concept in her deep despair. Then my heart remembered that Hatem's wife had given birth to their son, Hadi, only a few months before, and I said, "Who will teach Hatem's tiny son about his father? Who knows Hatem's story from the moment of his birth?

Only you, Ulwiya. You must live to teach him of his noble father. No one, not even his mother, can do that like you can."

Nearly four years later, in the summer of 1998, I visited Ulwiya, the loving grandmother of that little boy, who had come to spend the day with her. I wondered if she remembered our conversation when she said to me:

He is too young for me to teach him much about his father, but I expect to do that in the years ahead. For now, he comes and is happy playing here with me.

He was learning love in the same way Hatem had learned it—at Ulwiya's knee. The value of a close, loving family was spilling over into the life of this handsome little boy in the next generation.

Before Hatem's death, Ulwiya learned that she also had cancer. During her son's last months, she sometimes found herself taking him to his doctor at one hospital and then going to see her own doctor at another hospital. Having survived the loss of her husband and facing now the approaching loss of their son as well as her own life-threatening diagnosis, she had to decide once again to opt for life rather than give in to death. To say that she had taken this decision wholeheartedly would not have been true.

She had chosen the option of chemotherapy and was well into it when next we met. I was in Jerusalem for only a few weeks, and by sheer serendipity I phoned her on a day she was there, too. She was living near Athens, Greece, with her daughter, Nawar, who cared for her between trips to Jerusalem for the chemotherapy treatments. Ulwiya was in Jerusalem to see the doctor and was about to return to Greece with Nawar but was still in town for a day.

When I called, she invited me to walk the short distance from the hotel where I was staying so that we could have a brief visit in that wonderful house she loved so much and had managed to maintain through all her recent troubles.

She greeted me with a kerchief over her hairless head. There she stood, my slight little friend who was now even thinner. Dark circles

surrounded her lovely eyes. As we embraced, she was light as a feath-
er. Immediately I noticed that all the furniture was covered with
sheets except on the sun porch—our favorite spot to sit and visit
under her flourishing hoya plant.

There was the unmistakable aroma of anise seed tea brewing. I
knew it took some time and no little effort to brew my favorite drink.
Was she thinking this might be our last visit? Nawar and I became
acquainted as we sipped from the same tiny cups Ulwiya and I had
drunk from during our interview all those years ago. Soon her mother's treatments would be finished—and the doctors expected a successful outcome—but in the meantime she would be staying with
Nawar in Greece.

It was a brief but surprisingly pleasant visit. I felt encouraged
about Ulwiya's condition but longed to be able to somehow cheer her
through this illness. It occurred to me that my friend Diodora, a
Greek-Orthodox nun who was then near Athens, could visit her. I
knew that it would be her joy to do it.

I wrote to Diodora about Ulwiya, explaining that I had had only
a brief visit with her and was worried about her emaciated body but
more about her despondent mood. I asked that she call on Ulwiya
and try to lift her spirits. She wrote me later of the tender time they
had shared.

Now Ulwiya's cancer is in remission. Her lovely silver hair has
grown back, and little by little she is regaining some of the lost
weight. More wonderful than that, her smile is back, as is the energy
behind her gentle manner and loving ways. She is such a blessing to
all who know her. She cheers others again, just as she cheered me in
my Jerusalem days.

She spoke once of spontaneous prayers, beyond the memorized
lines from the Koran:

We call it "duha," which means just to call God, as if you are
talking to God. It's different than a prayer, it's a conversation ask-
ing for help and mercy and so on.

How many times in the years I have known her she has called for God. Sometimes she felt the heavens were brass over her head, yet she painfully clung to her faith. We often spoke of feeling peace in the midst of whatever circumstance we might be in. She said once, upon meeting a leader from my church:

There was such a peace about him; he was full of a special spirit. I felt a serenity and calmness that touched my soul—a deep, pure religion felt in the heart, relaxing and nice.

Ulwiya searches for this deeply felt peace. It has been a lifelong quest and has brought her from homes in many lands, full circle, back to her home in Jerusalem. Her life has been full of losses, yet she does her best to add to the lives of others.

She made sure our children and grandchildren had Ramadan sweets when we visited Jerusalem for Christmas in December 1997. She came to our family party and beamed at the spectacle of nineteen Madsens, singing Christmas carols and lighting our Christmas pudding, so that all present might share the light we were feeling. It shone in her eyes.

A deeply religious person, Ulwiya never flaunts her belief but lives it daily and allows all around her their own brand of faith. With each encounter she teaches many lessons. For example, she says, "When I have a problem and something is troubling me, after prayer I am relaxed and I feel that the burden weighs a little bit less."

Hopefully she has pushed away her own cancer by applying her fragile will, medicine, and prayer. Watching her struggle against the walls that unexpectedly loomed in her life, one cannot help but be strengthened and blessed. In a life where joy seemed to escape her at every turn, she has known true happiness:

What makes me happiest? I have pondered so long about this question. You made me search deep down in my heart and soul. I discovered there that it is the love of people. I do love people and somehow I can discover what's good in a person and love him or her. I think people feel this love, and the reward is wonderful.

There is another thing that makes me happy now. It is the love of nature. The other day I saw a bird standing next to my window on a branch of the rose bush. It was shining. Its feathers were a lovely greenish-black beautiful color. It stood there, and I thought it was looking at me. It was singing. I wondered if the bird really enjoyed the scent of a flower; did it see the colors as lovely as we see them?

What a joy God gave us in nature, in all living things, human, animal and plants. All God's creatures are worth loving. Life makes me happy.

Then she added:

My understanding of my husband made me very happy. Living together and understanding each other. Of course, that doesn't mean we never had a quarrel or we never disagreed. It's good to work hard in the beginning on your marriage so that you will have a good end.

Everything depends upon equality. When people feel equal there will be peace. Our tradition says that a man gets a double inheritance. But with my children, boys and girls will inherit equally.

In the circle of Ulwiya's friends and family, all have received equally, bountifully, long before her property is divided. Perhaps this generous quality in her helps others learn they can quiet themselves in her pattern. It is not an easy peace but a hard-earned serenity. Her example engenders courage to be peaceful when everything goes against it.

Notes

1. Fatima al Zahra'a. *Fatima* means "the flower."
2. Sharon Rosen lives in Baka now. See chapter on Sharon Rosen.
3. Ulwiya recalls about Dr. Eddy, "I think he also worked in the oil business in Saudi Arabia associated with private companies or the Saudi government."
4. Equivalent to the Red Cross.
5. Al-Quds is the Arab name for Jerusalem.
6. Memorial Book compiled for Hatem Husseini, 1995. See "Medical College Will Succeed,"*Jerusalem Times,* November 11, 1994.

6. MARY FRANJI

In 1967 when I saw the nurses standing all dressed up, I said, "What's happening?" They said, "We're going home. There's war between Egypt and Jordan and Israel." I said, "No one goes home! We have children here, children who are very sick. We have to find a place to put them in."

Mary Franji

Anna Grace Lind and I trudged up the hill from Herod's Gate in the Old City. It was a pleasant day in 1993 with a small breeze blowing through the Arab quarter. She was taking me to the Spafford Children's Center. The cobblestone way steepened, but she was vigorous and even at age eighty-eight rarely slowed her pace. A smiling Arab woman stopped her just at the corner of the stone wall where we turned to go to the Center. As they chatted amiably in Arabic, I wondered just what Mary Franji would be like. She had been the head nurse at the Spafford Children's Center for many years, and I was going to meet her for the first time.

I was ill prepared for the tiny woman in a starched white nurse's uniform who rushed up to us as we arrived. One had the feeling she had only paused for a moment in mid-flight or, paradoxically, that she was about to take off! A hummingbird came to mind. Her close-cropped gray hair was the trademark of this totally practical little woman. She and Anna Grace were about the same height, but where Anna Grace was slight in build, Mary was round and healthy looking with rosy cheeks. Her smile grew even brighter as she recognized Anna Grace. There was a comfortable feeling between them, obviously the product of a lengthy, amiable association. She happily paused to greet the older woman. After introductions, Anna Grace busied herself with her own agenda and left me to mine.

Anna Grace had explained to me about Mary's beginnings:

Mary Franji has an interesting background. She is an Armenian, and her father and mother were killed in an army massacre when she was a little girl. She was taken by the missionaries who were there helping. They took her and put her in a nursery school of some type, an orphanage or something.

She was in this orphanage in Beirut, and when she got in her teens she decided that she was going to become a nurse. She came to Jerusalem and went to the English hospital here to train. [It was where the Anglican school is now.] When she graduated, she got a job in the St. John's hospital, near the railway station. The day that she got her job was the day the 1948 war started, and she couldn't find her way there while the fighting was going on. She decided she'd come to Mother [Bertha Spafford Vester] in the clinic and asked, "Do you want a nurse?" My mother threw her an apron and said, "Get to work." And she has been there ever since.

The outlines of this history were mostly correct, but my purpose was to fill in the details with Mary herself. As she showed me through the building the day of our first meeting, she said over her shoulder without a wasted motion, "I am Mary Franji, I am the supervisor here at the Spafford Center. Since 1948 I am with them. Even before the State [Israel]."

Her English had only a trace of an accent that sounded to me as if it had a Scottish or Irish edge to it. Perhaps it was the upward turn in her voice, the lilt. I would not have guessed she was of Armenian descent.

As we rushed along the hallway, she told me about assisting in an operating room when the Israelis came in 1967. She saw no reason to hurry the surgery or to leave just because there was a war beginning. I couldn't help commenting, "You have the spirit of Mrs. Vester!" We had just passed a lovely portrait of Bertha Spafford Vester in the clean but deteriorating hallway. Mary was obviously complimented but fended it off by acting as though I hadn't said anything.

I asked her if we might sit somewhere for a while so I could learn more about her life, even though it seemed an imposition to take her away from her tasks. She was not the sort who looked for an excuse to leave her work for a break.

We found a quiet room on the main floor, closed the door against the bustle of nurses, mothers, and children, and sat facing each other. It was easy to talk with her. There was not one moment of awkwardness between us. I felt we were instant friends.

Once we were sitting down, the words tumbled out, Mary relishing the recollection of dramatic incidents long past. She colored her account with so many details that I could easily picture the scenes she described. When she took a breath, I seized the opportunity to ask her to start at the beginning.

She did.

*I was born in Beirut, Lebanon, on June 28, 1923. At least that is
what my passport says. But I think that I am younger than that.
They made identity cards for us at the boarding school, but they
weren't really sure, so they put 1923.*

*My father had died in Turkey in a massacre of Armenians
there. My family had been living in Turkey. They had moved
there from Armenia.*

*My mother died in Lebanon when I was less than two years
old and I don't remember her, I only remember my grandmother.
Her name was Kahani. The name means "maiden" in Turkish. It
seems she was ladylike or something. I remember a little of her,
but then I was put in a kind of boarding school.*

*I must have been five or six when I went to the boarding
school. I lived in Beirut until 1944 when I was about twenty-one
years old. The director in the school arranged for me to come to
the English mission hospital in Jerusalem because I wanted to be
a nurse. That's how I came to Jerusalem.*

*I was trained for four years in the English hospital, the mis-
sion to the Jews, which is the Anglican School now. It was during
the British Mandate. It was a regular nursing course, and we
worked hard there. We really learned the basics of bedside nursing. Later, when I was studying in the States, the doctors used to
say, "Where is that Jerusalem nurse who knows bedside nursing?"*

*Our patients at the English Hospital were Jews, and there
were Arabs, too. When it was time for food in that hospital, the
Arabs used to bring their chairs to sit with their neighbor, the
patient next door. There was no ill feeling. Each group had its
own kitchen; the Jews had their kosher kitchen, and the Arabs
had their kitchen. There was a lovely, peaceful feeling.*

*We worked then with Israeli Jewish nurses. Later [1949] I
sent food to my Jewish friends, who were on the other side. The
Israelis didn't have food at the beginning. I sent some food with
the UN observers. There was nothing coming between us, we*

loved each other, we worked together, we covered for each other. If the night nurse forgot something, we, the day nurses, did it quickly, so the sister wouldn't see and wake her up. You know they were very strict, real bedside nursing.

She said this with such pride. Her confidence in her ability to bless by her ministrations was obvious and well deserved.

When the Israelis took over the hospital and the nurses' training was stopped, Mary went to do private nursing for the Reverend Eric Bishop:

He had a broken leg and I was looking after him in the hospital before it closed, so he chose me to go home with him. He was living in the Swedish Language School on Prophets' Street, that interesting house with green shutters.

I stayed there a while with him and his wife. They offered to send me to study medicine. I said that I didn't have the background. I told them I'd like to be a midwife, and so they were arranging for me, but the immigration department was closed here and that plan didn't work.

Immigration offices seem to be closed more often than they are open in the Middle East. But Mary was resourceful. She knew her services would be needed somewhere in a Jerusalem being threatened by war. The war itself changed her plans and the direction she would take the rest of her life:

I decided to go to St. John's open hospital, which is on the way to Bethlehem. I went to see the matron there. She asked me, "Can you start now?" I asked her if she would give me a week to rest. She said, "Yes, just leave your things here." So I left my things. After a few days I heard that that area had been taken by the Israelis, so I couldn't go.

I stayed by Jaffa Gate in Christ's Church. It was very cheap, and it was connected with the English mission. While I was there, I heard that Mrs. Vester needed a nurse.

*I went to see her and reminded her of when I had nursed her
and that she had never liked me because I was small. But she said
that if I was from the English mission hospital she must like me,
because the nurses there were good nurses and that she didn't
need to see any references. Then she gave me a present. She said,
"You must always say I'm small but good." During the next years
when she would meet me she would say, "Oh Mary, you're my little nurse!"*

When she began working for Mrs. Vester, her work was mostly at
the old Spafford home, on the northern wall of the Old City, which
had been turned into a hospital for children. She is such a fixture
there now that it is hard to visualize her seeing it for the first time:

*I didn't know this place. I had never seen it. Mrs. Vester sent me
with a young man, an Arab worker from the American Colony.
We walked, and we hardly saw a cat or a bird or anyone. The
streets were just wiped of anyone. It was so isolated that I got a
little nervous being with this young man, never knowing these
streets.*

*So when I came in it was all garden, beautiful flowers, such
a beautiful place. I was so much taken with it. I could not believe
that here was supposed to be my home.*

Mary moved in and began working. In a week Mrs. Vester sent a
man with a note (there were no telephones): "Mary, please come."
She left another Armenian nurse to look after things and went to help
Mrs. Vester, who had bought a quantity of medical instruments and
supplies from the British Army Hospital, which was then at Augusta
Victoria, on the Mount of Olives:

*I looked at it [all the medical instruments] and, of course, there
was nothing sterile so I put some water in a saucepan, and put a
strainer inside with gauze and cotton to sterilize with steam. The
British High Commission had given Mrs. Vester six gallons of*

kerosene before they left. It was very precious. It is amazing what
God gives and how He arranges it.

How He arranges it is the amazing part. Mrs. Vester took Mary
under her wing, and it was there at the American Colony that Mary
met her future husband. One wonders if Hanna Franji wasn't party to
an arranged marriage that began in the mind and heart of Bertha:

Hanna Franji worked at the American Colony, and we met there.
He was fifteen years older than I was but single, never having
been married. He was an Arab but he was loved by the Jews, by
the Muslims, by the Christians—everyone. His friends were the
porters and the poor people.

I really loved him because he was so good. Money meant
nothing to him. He was always helping people. I knew him from
1948 and we were married in 1954. In between, I went to the
States. He asked me before to marry him but I said I'm going now
to America.

Mary still hoped to improve her medical education. This time no
closed immigration office kept her from it:

Mrs. Vester sent me in 1951 to take a postgraduate course in
the United States. So when I went there, she had a friend who
was working in public relations who felt me to be her responsi-
bility. They thought, "Here is someone coming from the Orient.
She will be such a burden to us." But I was no burden to anybody.

Mrs. Vester sent me to Boston to the Baptist Hospital, but
then I thought, why not go to the Children's Hospital? It was next
to Harvard University. They were all surprised, Mrs. Vester and
all, but I said, "I am coming back to a children's hospital so I
wanted somewhere to train for that."

It was such fun comparing notes on Mary's time in Boston. I had
lived for nine years in Boston, and my daughter Emily, who happened

to be visiting during the time I interviewed Mary, had been born at the Boston Lying-in Hospital near the same Children's Hospital where Mary had trained. Mary obviously loved her time in America. Everything was new to her, but she was able to fend for herself in this new and challenging medical world.

> Just after I arrived, the people asked me, "Did you learn your English here?" I would answer, "How could I? I've only been a week here. I am not so genius."

She knew well how to nurse and therefore was well within her comfort zone doing it. Her goal was to be the best nurse around.

> I lived in Good Samaritan House near the hospital. The doctors used to say, "Where is the Jerusalem girl who knows bedside nursing?" When they had really sick children, they liked me there.
>
> We worked sometimes twenty-four hours a day during our training. We really worked hard. I had good experience there. Then I asked the American Nurses Association could they send me somewhere in the poorer section because I'm not going to work in a "bed of roses," I'm going back to Jerusalem. So they were very nice; they sent me to Michael Reese Hospital in the slums of Chicago. I didn't know it was a Jewish hospital.
>
> In Chicago there were many blacks and they were very religious. They used to say, "Did you really come from Jerusalem? Can I touch you?" And they thought I was sainted. And I thought to myself, they are being deceived, I am only a human being.
>
> "Miss K.," they used to call me. My name was Kahkajian. Armenian is always "ian" at the end. Armenians were some of the first Christians in the world. And we suffered a lot. They used to ask me in England, "Do they still wear grass skirts where you live?" And I said, "When you were running after the deer, our nation fought for Christianity."
>
> I met a really good group in the hospital: Swedish nurses whose ancestors had come to Minnesota and Hawaiian girls and

Hanna and Mary

Dutch girls. They were very surprised to find someone from Jerusalem.

I asked Mary what happened to her friendship with Hanna Franji while she was in America, and she said, "We used to write." Still curious, I asked boldly if they were love letters. She laughed and said, "I suppose so."

On her return to Jerusalem after three years of training in America, she found that the love letters had done their work. The courtship resumed.

I was married in 1954. When we went to tell Mrs. Vester that we were going to get married, she said to Hanna, my husband, "You are marrying a tiger." And I said we didn't come to discuss that. He knows that, I said. She said that because I used to tell her what I thought. I used to tell her my ideas. I thought this was the right way, I just did what was right.

> *She used to like me. "Oh, Mary," she'd say, "I wish I was young like you." And now I think I know what that means.*

Mary had a call from Hanna the morning of their wedding day. She had already learned to prize his honesty. She had spoken of people in today's world who lie and try to cover up, but Hanna was so straightforward and she found that "so lovely."

> *He called me up at 9:30 A.M. and he said, "You still have time. I'm much older than you and I don't have money. If you want to change your mind . . ." At 10 A.M. we were married.*
>
> *Our wedding was at the Dominican Church. And Mrs. Vester arranged that we have our reception at the Pasha Room at the American Colony.[1]*

She continued with details of the reception:

> *For a present she gave us a beautiful carpet. And Mrs. Lind arranged a beautiful table with cards with the names of the people who had been invited. She had painted the cards with white flowers, so beautiful that I have kept them till now. Mrs. Lind also arranged with the cook to have a delicious wedding cake.*

The wedding marked the beginning of a happy time for Mary. She loved this man who had given her every opportunity not to marry him:

> *Hanna was wonderful. There was no government for six weeks [between the British Mandate and the new Israeli government]. You had to be a very understanding type because the irregular soldiers wanted to take over and destroy the Colony. You know how soldiers are. My husband had a nice way, he used to give them cigarettes and feed them from the Colony to try to win them. You have to have a nice way. This daughter of mine who is a social worker, she has his ways.*

"And your ways, too," I assured Mary. I had met her daughter Shoshana, who was thirty-five at the time and lived with her mother. She also worked at the Spafford Center, where she was in charge of the social work. When I asked if she thought Shoshana would ever marry, Mary said her daughter was married to her work. She told me more about this giving daughter of hers:

I'm more strict, I think, than Shoshana. Sometimes we used to give old clothes to the charity cases, and I used to put in a bag and give. Shoshana got very upset and said, "No, Mother, let them choose. They have the right to choose. Just because they can't pay . . ." This was the practical part, why lose time, without paying anything. The others who could afford used to pay one shekel for one piece.

Do you think I can ever get anything from her about her patients? Never one word of the good she does. But the other day one of her fellow social workers called me up and said, "Are you the mother? You must be so proud. You know those patients who are so miserable, how she treats them. They tell us she's the angel of this world."

It was easy to see that like mother, like daughter, though neither would own up to the incredible amount of good they did. I was glad I had met Shoshana on many occasions. And I was curious about the older daughter, Lydia, who was married and lived in Canada with Mary's three grandchildren. Mary told me:

I bring Lydia from Canada every year so that she won't lose her identity card. She is named after Hanna's mother. She was born in 1955, and Shoshana was born in 1958. I took off three months after each was born.

Then I had to find someone to care for them. I found a Jewish baby nurse who was married to a Muslim. She had two daughters. Her husband had been married before and the first wife came and said, "She doesn't give you any sons. Why don't you take me back?" And he did.

Poor girl, she didn't know what to do. She took care of my children. She was so good.

One day, after the girls were older, Hanna took his wife and daughters to see the house where he had grown up in Jerusalem. His father had come from Lebanon, but his mother was from Jerusalem. They had lived in a house where Israelis now live, on Agron St. next to the American Consulate in the Mamilla section of the city.

Hanna took me to see his sister and then he said, "I'll show you my house?" So we went and he knocked on the door and a Jewish woman came out. He said, "I'm Hanna. I just want to show my wife this is where we grew, this is our house. Do you mind if I show her?" She was so kind. She said, "Yes, come in."

So he showed where his bedroom was, where his bed sat, where they used to play in a park opposite where there was a swimming pool where they swam. He told all that to his children. It was so nice. They were so gracious to us. He said to them, "Thank you very much for showing us." The Jewish woman said, "This is war, but I'm sorry they've taken your house."

The years that followed were busy, productive years. The little Franji family of four got on well. But after only fifteen years of marriage, in 1969 Mary's husband died of cancer, not long after her mentor, Bertha Spafford Vester, had died.

I remember when my husband had cancer and he was operated on at Hadasseh Ein Kerem Hospital. I needed to go somewhere to pray, and I found the synagogue and I went in. I prayed. It's a prayer house. This is what I feel. My husband was that kind of man, too.

He died on June 23, 1969. The 24th was his name day, St. John's Day. He was buried on his name day on Mt. Zion in the Catholic cemetery.

Mary continued at the Spafford and gave herself to raising her two girls. She was so glad they were old enough to have known and to be able to remember their father. I almost felt I knew him as well, because she spoke of him so glowingly, always suggesting that the good qualities in her daughters were traceable to him.

I wondered who her friends might have been and what kind of support system she had had in those years while she was rearing her daughters as a single parent.

Mary learned giving by watching and doing. But it is easy to believe that her indomitable spirit came equipped to give:

> Sometimes I talk to women who play bridge all the time, and they say that they are fed up with their lives. I say, "Why? There is so much to do. Why don't you go and help in these poor homes of mercy? There are so many old people."
>
> I first went there, to see one of our workers who was sick. I used to ask that they would take me there so we can take something to the old people. And when I get there, everyone pulling me, "Me, too! Me, too!" My tears were running. Why not, why not go do that? Why play bridge. What is bridge? Why do people sit like vegetables and watch TV? I think it's a sin.

Mary explained to me the philosophy at the Center that was in place long before she arrived. Anna Spafford, whose name her daughter Bertha had given to the Center, came to Jerusalem precisely to give help wherever and to whomever needed. She quickly found objects for her charitable helping. From her time to the present, it could have been said just as Mary repeated it to me:

> We do not preach here at the Spafford. We feel that this "not preaching" is what Mrs. Vester would have done, and all the Vester family have the idea that you show your faith in your life.

And how would Mary describe her faith? What brings her peace?

When I can be useful. And I thank God every morning that I can stand on my feet, that I can climb these stairs to be useful and that is how we have to look upon it. People see in your life. Your life should be a picture.

It was easy to agree with Mary. She was so upbeat, so full of good intentions. I wondered if she was ever disappointed in the people she lived among—the Palestinians, the Israelis. She was. But she was also full of hope because of her own history, the experiences she had had when there was regular laughter between Arab and Jew.

Both sides here can live in peace. When they were building the sewage system, when the Israelis came into the municipality, both Arabs and Jews were working together. I used to give them tea outside. And you should see the laughter of the two. I keep on saying to everyone, it's only the big shots from both sides who want to be in the highest chairs. That disturbs matters. Otherwise, simple people could live. The longer it stays like this, the longer the hatred will increase. That's so sad.

One day I asked Mary if she had known Hind Husseini. She brightened visibly and said she had known her since 1948. When orphans were sent to the Spafford, she said they would send them to Hind. When Hind had sick children, she would send them to the Spafford, where there were doctors, because it was a hospital in those days.

We took care of her children free because she was doing good work. Our doctor sees them, and we don't charge them for medications, although we are struggling, [but we did that] because she was doing a wonderful work. Any child that came to her she took in. It made no difference if they were Muslim or Christian. If they were children, she took them. Just like here at Spafford. We have no difference, whoever comes is welcome.

I used to go see her. We had a lot in common. We talked about our troubles. She was always cheerful. She could have had money herself but she put all her money in the work.

Yes, a lot in common. Hind and Mary remained friends over the years and met for the last time in the waiting room of a doctor only a few weeks before Hind's death.

I met her in St. John's Hospital. Someone put a hand on me and kissed me. I looked up. "Oh," I said, "my old friend." We sat down waiting our turn. She wants to give me her turn and I want to give her mine with the doctor. But we sat waiting for our turn. The English doctor was going to see us. St. John's is an eye hospital now. We had a lot to talk about. That was the last time I heard her say, "Oh Mary, we've had our share in this life. Joy and lots of sorrow. We saw lots of happy days." Accomplishment— she said the word "accomplishment."

I said to her that if there were ten women like her, the world would have been much better. Only ten. This part I know is true.

And Mary Franji would certainly be one of them!

We spoke of others she had known. She spoke in complimentary terms of everyone except the occasional youngster whom she supervised who "hadn't any idea how to work." I smiled when she explained that a young workman had taken two weeks to do what should have been finished in two hours. It would have taken only two hours if she had been put on the task!

But her memory of others was positive and even admiring.

I heard that your students go over and volunteer for Mrs. Majaj [at the Princess Basma Center for Disabled Children]. I know her and I know her husband, Dr. Majaj. In 1948 I met him. He never asked for money. I asked him, "How do you live? You see patients and you never ask for money." He said, "Money is not everything." He is the first man I ever heard say that.

Mary's heart is filled with memories of Bertha Spafford Vester and her daughter Anna Grace Lind. Both were her mentors. Her loyalty to them transcends personal discomfort—she never really thinks of her-

Anna Grace and Mary

self as ill, so there have been few absences from her post over the years. Recently when she fell, hurting her leg, she still managed to hobble around, directing the traffic of the Center because they needed her. She spoke to me of Bertha's last birthday celebration:

> *I remember her putting her hand on my husband's face, "Hanna, what would I have done without you?" And she kissed me and said, "Mary, you're here. I want you to be here."*
>
> *Anna Grace said the same thing. She said to me, "Don't leave that place, Mary." And I assured her time and time again that I wouldn't. I say to God, "Give me strength!" And He does.*
>
> *I promised Anna Grace that I would look after things here, and I will as long as I have breath.*

The year 1998 marked Mary Franji's fiftieth year at the Spafford Center. The Spafford newsletter featured her. "Happy 50th Anniversary to Mary Franji" shouts the headline, accompanied by an early photo of—what else?—Mary holding a baby. There is also a more recent photo of Mary with another baby and a lovely third picture with her good friend Anna Grace Lind. Next to the one with Anna Grace is the verse from Proverbs 17:17: "A friend loveth at all times . . ." The printed tribute speaks of Mary's sharing with hundreds "her memories of the Center's early days and also her personal memories of the Jerusalem of her youth." It ends:

> We rejoice in her continued presence at the Center. It just wouldn't be the same without her!! [Then Georgette Lind adds a personal note.] Peter and I would like to say a special "thank you" to Mary for her devotion to Anna Grace.

What has brought her to this milestone in her life? Certainly not long vacations near the sea nor relaxing travels abroad whenever the pace was too hurried. On the contrary, the pace has always been too hurried, and I doubt she knows the meaning of the word *vacation*. Instead, she has given herself wholeheartedly to "the children"—the many, many children like those she reminded the other nurses about at the beginning of the 1967 war, "No one goes home! We have children here, children who are very sick."

Notes

1. The Pasha Room still exists in the American Colony Hotel. It had actually been the lavish bedroom of the pasha who first lived there. Its ceiling is a blue canopy with stars, and the other appointments in the room are sumptuous and reminiscent of that earlier luxurious day. It could not have been much less lavish for Mary's wedding reception.

7. Betty Majaj

When my son was nearly ten years old, a Jewish lady
came to visit us [a rare occurrence, because the
Majaj family are Arab and live in East Jerusalem].
The Jewish lady was my sister's mother-in-law. I was
afraid that my son might say something to hurt or
embarrass her. So, I taught my son. I said, "You
know, we have a Jewish lady coming to spend a few
days with us. She's Jewish, but she is family."

Betty Majaj

The first time I walked into her garden I remembered my Palestinian friend, Betty Majaj, telling me of her son fashioning jasmine petals into a necklace for a Jewish visitor:

> *It was summer. We were sitting outside on the patio, and the ground was covered with jasmine flowers. Saleh, my little son, went into the room, got a needle and a thread. I didn't know what he was doing, and I was busy, you know, very anxious to meet her and talk to her. She was a Cohen, one of the important tribes of Israel. He sat at our feet, threading those jasmines and making a necklace. We hardly noticed him. He didn't care. He didn't mind, Jew or not Jew, she was family. Immediately when he finished it, he came and put it over her neck.*
>
> *As she was dying in Haifa, I went to see her. She reminded me of that story on her deathbed, how my son only cared that she was family. It didn't matter what the Jews did to the Arabs.*

When Betty Majaj told me this lovely story of acceptance, she might have been thinking to explain to me how peace can come when we all think of each other as family. She might have been describing her son's innocent responses or showing how long the "Jewish lady" remembered the olive branch presented as a jasmine lei, or perhaps showing how trust is natural in children.

Whatever she was thinking, what I heard was how a mother teaches a child to love, for *family* to Betty Majaj was synonymous with *love*. And with love in place, hatred is automatically discarded:

> *Hatred will slowly, slowly disappear, naturally, spontaneously, because people are not born with it. And they are not taught to hate by their religion. No religion teaches hatred, not the Muslim, nor Christian, nor Jew.*

That is the way Betty sees it. Others among whom she lives somehow learn to hate with a kind of everlasting hatred that predates their own experience. They can't remember just when the hate-snake first

Betty with Jerusalem Center ladies and quilts
Malak Sharaf, Ann Madsen, Charlotte Cundick

bit, but its poisonous venom continues from one generation to the next. Individuals in all camps can be observed collecting offenses day after month after year. It is a sordid task, but some think it essential. Betty's credo precludes such collecting.

I first met Betty in her official role as director of the Princess Basma Disabled Children's Center. One thing I noticed immediately was her kindness, her courtesy, an innate gentleness. She is a woman of peace in every sense of the word.

I had crossed the ridge of the Mount of Olives from Hebrew University into the village of E-Tur to meet the director of the Princess Basma Center. Students from the Jerusalem Center for Near Eastern Studies, where I taught, went there regularly to help with the children. I was expecting to meet a Palestinian, but she did not look Palestinian to me. I was confused.

When we met in 1997, Betty was a handsome seventy-year-old woman, vibrant and obviously well educated. She was a stately, immaculately groomed executive with genuine charisma. The few lines in her face traced a lifetime of smiles. She had not always had a tranquil life, but her native optimism had carried her along. Laughter came easily to her, and the cultural differences between us disappeared in our joking together. She was clearly a strong woman, a woman of influence willing to wield whatever power she had to do good.

She hated to waste time. She viewed the world as a workplace and referred to herself as a workaholic. She was unafraid to tackle the most challenging task, as her direction of the Princess Basma Center demonstrated.

Betty was born in 1927 in Sidon, a city in Lebanon that has survived from antiquity and is usually mentioned in the same breath as Tyre. They were the main cities of ancient Phoenicia.

When I asked if her real name was Elizabeth, she said:

No, it is Betty—actually, Betty Barbara, because I was born on December 4, St. Barbara's Day. I have two names because, being raised as a Catholic, I had to have a saint's name when I was baptized. My name is Betty Barbara Dagher Majaj.

I spent my early childhood in Sidon in an American boarding school. That's where my mother got my name. She had been friendly with an American teacher whose name was Betty. She named me after her, whereas my sister and my two brothers were given Arabic names.

One of Betty's brothers is a vascular surgeon and chief of staff in a Washington, D.C., hospital. The other serves as dean of the Agricultural Department of the Emirates in the Gulf area and is presently at the American University of Beirut. Her only sister died at age twenty-three.

Betty lives in the busy downtown section of East Jerusalem. Yet, as one enters her home through a green door and walks down a passageway into a lovely courtyard brimming with vines and flowers, it is difficult to believe there is any city bustle outside the walls. It is such a restful, quiet spot, inviting one to relax for a while and sip a tall, cool glass of freshly made lemonade with a slight aftertaste of rosewater. At the right season, there is the heavy odor of jasmine, with blossoms snowing down all around.

Betty came first to Jerusalem as a bride in 1947, "just before the troubles here," or the Israeli War of Independence:

> *The British were about to leave. I didn't have the chance to know Palestine then, but my husband was Palestinian and he has always lived here. We met when he was doing his medical study and I was doing my nursing study at the American University in Beirut [Lebanon]. When we met, I was eighteen and a half. I finished my nursing training at the age of nineteen. I was very young. They didn't like to accept anyone [to be trained] who was less than eighteen, but they needed Arab nurses. There were before mostly Armenians, Polish, Jews who went in for this career, and nursing was still looked upon as a degrading profession.*

Beirut was the showplace of the Middle East as recently as 1968. The university and the city were modern, clean, full of flowers. It was easy to picture Amin and Betty learning to love each other in that elegant city. It was not as easy to picture her returning to the sad, burned-out place it had become by the 1990s.

> *I go every year to Beirut, in spite of the war. My mother is still living in West Beirut. This was considered the Muslim side, but we never thought of the Muslim side and the Christian side.*

The Muslim side? The Christian side? What did she mean?

I recalled walking in Beirut with my husband in 1968. We met only one man that evening, and he spoke to us easily in English. We had been puzzled by the Muslim-Christian partnership in the country and asked him to explain it. He told us that they divided power between them equally. He gave details of how the parliament regulated affairs and explained a system of checks and balances that involved the president and prime minister. It all sounded perfectly reasonable. Everything seemed orderly and safe in beautiful Beirut.

That evening, as we bade our new friend farewell, it surprised me to hear him say that someday there would be a terrible civil war in Lebanon. I asked why, when such a sane and workable system seemed in place and the two groups had maintained a peaceful coexistence for some time. He gave no reason but kept repeating that one day there would be chaos in this beautiful city. He advised us to look around carefully because it would never be the same. I wonder if he has lived to see his prophecy so precisely fulfilled.

Thinking of Betty's mother living in the shell that is present-day Beirut was painful. Betty explained that her mother had had a few bad moments during the war there but no problems involving religion. When the war was at its worst, she fled to her son's home in the United States and lived with his family.

My father died in '83, and then, in '87, when there was the infil-tration of the Israeli army into Lebanon [the area the Israelis call their security zone] the Christian towns east of Sidon were all demolished. The first house was my father's house. They just demolished everything. Luckily, my mother was living in Beirut proper, but then her brother-in-law, my uncle, became homeless completely, so he and his wife came and lived with her. Now . . . she is eighty-four, and can't be on her own. They still live with her.

I go each year to see her. It's not easy for her to come here because the Israelis have a law preventing all women over sixty-five and widows to come as visitors [evidently from fear they will remain]. But we have a very good contact—a nice Jewish man helped me—and I was able to get her here last year for Christmas. This year I didn't try because it was too cold. I use the southern road, the Metulla Road, and it's not really safe now in the winter season.

Through so much of what Betty said were references to her friendly relationships with many Jews. As a deeply religious mother, she had made sure that hatred was never part of her children's vocab-ulary. Surely Betty's deep belief in the teachings of Jesus about loving enemies has influenced her interaction with all those among whom she lives.

Other examples of that ongoing interaction revolve around a Jewish violin teacher:

> I remember after the '67 war that among the first people we received were my husband's best friend, his violin teacher, a Jew. He was very, very grand. He didn't want to come. He didn't know how we were going to receive them. He sent us a priest with a message that said, "I feel with you. Please tell me if you need any money. I know you are cut off completely." We were cut off. We didn't know how we were going to reach banks to get money. He then said, "I can spare so much money. If you need it, please tell me. If you don't, just forget about it."
>
> And then, who else came? My father-in-law's Jewish partner in his business. All these people knew what an Arab was. They had lived with Arabs. They dressed like Arabs. But now we don't expect the same from the young in the Zionist movement. Some of them have never met an Arab. They are afraid to talk to an Arab. They are afraid to see an Arab. It's building up more and more hatred on both sides.[1]

Betty's daughter Randa recalled that as children, she and her brother and sisters would visit the YMCA near the Mandelbaum Gate. There they could peek over the wall separating Jews from Arabs in the divided Jerusalem. They would stand on tiptoe, "hoping a Jew would walk by so we could see what they looked like." Real familiarity can eventually foster friendship; knowing little or nothing about someone often breeds fear and distrust.

The business partner of Betty's father-in-law, a trusted friend, also came to their aid during the 1967 war. She remembers:

> My husband is always telling me that his father's partner was a Jew. His father would hand Amin, my husband, five hundred Palestinian pounds to deliver to his partner, Moshe. He was to

give him the money. My husband would ask, "Father, should I ask for a receipt?" His father would answer, "What, a receipt? Moshe is enough."

The story brought back memories of my first trip to Jerusalem in 1968 when I met Jews and Arabs mingling together, laughing and talking. They were friends. No other word would describe the situation. I exclaimed to Betty, "I have seen it like that. Can it ever be like that again?"

We hope so. Everyone who remembers is hoping it will be like that again. It takes time to build mutual confidence and trust. If mothers feel it, they will naturally convey it to their children. The attitudes of mothers will make a big difference. It will come with a general sense of security and justice and normal living. We haven't had normal living for so long.

She knew whereof she spoke. As a mother, she had had to decide what to teach her children, and she had quietly taught them of peace by being peaceful. She had offered them the gift of a happy, carefree childhood. Her daughter Randa speaks of that time as idyllic, with no cares. Ironically, a few sentences later, Randa describes being eight years old and trapped in their East Jerusalem home during the 1967 war:

On the first day of the war, I remember that someone picked us up from school and rushed us home. When I came in, Mom was hurriedly assembling supplies in the kitchen for a first-aid kit. When the shooting started, she gathered the four children, the housekeeper, and an old lady who had strayed in off the street not understanding what was happening. There was an inner hall where she spread out one mattress, and we all slept there and stayed there for the six days.

People knocked at our door as they were fleeing and asked us to go but my mom said no. Dad was still at Augusta Victoria

Hospital. We didn't know if he was all right, and he didn't know if we were. There are still bullet holes in our walls, and one in the front door.

The Jordanian army was stationed right around the corner from our house and had an anti-aircraft gun mounted which boomed periodically. We had no electricity. We had plenty of food because my mother always kept lots of food in the freezer. But when we heard bullets puncture the water tanks on the roof, Mom risked her life to rush into the kitchen to fill all the pots and pans so that we would have water. Otherwise it would all be wasted, draining out on the roof.

On the last day of the war, six days after we had hidden away, someone called from outside to come and look at all the dead [Jordanians]. As a naive child, I really wanted to go out to see all the dead bodies, not really understanding what I would see—having had no TV exposure—but my mother wouldn't let me. On the same day, my father hurried down our street to find partly collapsed houses of our neighbors and wondered if he could hope to find us alive. You can imagine the reunion when he found us huddled in our "safe place."

When Betty spoke of the role that families play in making peace, I asked her how children on either side can be taught to trust, to go beyond the distrust that has multiplied exponentially in recent years:

The most important thing now for families is to build a generation with good morals—you know, we've lost a lot of the morals in children. The parents lost control of their children. Children became very wild, very violent, very "self-minded" [burning tires, throwing stones, writing their ideas for all to see on the walls of the city]. So we have to build.

I think we have to start working on the parents themselves, not just in schools alone. Our schools are stressing very good ethics, good morals, good conduct in the schoolchildren. But it is

*important that we're starting also to strengthen the Parent
Teacher Association—to introduce all these ideas to the mothers.*

Betty Majaj has lived in Jerusalem exactly the length of time the
Israeli State has existed. Israelis view this period as a time of growth
in their economy and even their borders, because the Six Day War in
1967 added territory to their country. More important, it united both
halves of Jerusalem. Although the Israelis took possession of the city,
tearing down the barriers that had existed since 1948 and thinking to
unite the city once and for all, some said that there would always be
an invisible wall separating Israelis from Palestinians.

Ever since the first Intifada erupted in December 1987, that invisible wall has become a line drawn in the sand by both Palestinians
and Israelis, sometimes shifting, but always there. The Intifada was
characterized by merchants on strike in the Old City and rock-throw-
ing youth—often out of control.

Graffiti covers many of the gleaming white limestone walls,
ancient and modern, in greater Jerusalem. Black and red lines hurriedly drawn by youth in Hebrew or Arabic shout silently where
Israeli or Palestinian feels that invisible line should be.[2]

Betty Majaj first lived in Jerusalem when the line was drawn to
include the city as part of Jordan. This was the most productive,
happy time she remembers.

The Six Day War changed all of that. The uneasy occupation by
Israelis moved the line so that Jerusalem became a united Israeli city
with many *dunams* of expropriated land that had recently been owned
by Arabs and had once been governed by Jordan.[3] These areas became
known as the West Bank, referring to Jordan's holdings in what was
more and more often being referred to as Palestine, the name of a
hoped-for Arab state.

During much of this time, Amin Majaj, Betty's husband and a pediatrician, was director of the Makassed Hospital as well as medical director of Augusta Victoria Hospital on the Mount of Olives. Many knew
that he was also unofficial mayor of the Arab population of Jerusalem,
a part of the Arab shadow government whose moderates dreamed of

making East Jerusalem the capital of a future Palestinian state. Others, admittedly more extreme, hoped to claim all of Jerusalem. With both sides vowing never to give up Jerusalem, the deadlock remains.

The Majaj marriage began in a turbulent time. Amin was deeply involved in providing medical help when it was sorely needed in 1948. The British had just pulled out, leaving little infrastructure. The Israelis had declared themselves a state and won the war that consolidated their statehood on the international scene. Betty describes her husband's role in these challenging times:

> *It was in 1948 when the first war started. He was among the very few doctors who did not run away. He went to the Russian compound in Bethany. The Mother Superior was British. She and another nun came together on a boat as missionaries, and they ended being in charge of two convents. Mother Martha was in charge of the Bethany convent, and Mother Mary was in Gethsemane [just a few kilometers apart, one on the eastern slope of the Mount of Olives and one on the western side near the bottom of the mount].*
>
> *He went to Mother Martha and said, "Look, we have a war on our hands. We do not have enough hospitals. We need your help." There was only one hospital in the Old City, the Austrian hospital, which is now a hospice.*

Where was Betty while this was happening? She told the amazing story of being an Arab woman in Jerusalem in 1948:

> *We had been married for four months. Amin sent all the women—myself, my mother, my two sisters—and his other brother, who was not a medical man, to Lebanon. We went to my family, to my father's house, to get away from the war. Then Amin took stock, wondering what to do, how to help the people. He went to Mother Martha and asked her, "Would you give me the convent to turn it into a hospital for minor injuries, minor surgery?" She did that.*

He cabled me, "Come immediately. I need you," because he had no nurses. The novices were used as nurses at the time, and he didn't have one single qualified nurse. And I was there in Lebanon, already qualified, not knowing what to do. There was only at the time a six-seater plane to Lebanon.

His first telegram arrived, "Come immediately. I need you. We started a hospital, and you have to run the hospital." When the telegram arrived, I had renal colic. I was in bed. I couldn't answer back. I didn't know where to find a telegram station.

The second day, I didn't show up. The third day, he came to me and he found me in bed. I said, "We will go back." So I came back, and we arrived at this hospital with the nuns and novices.

We worked in Bethany for nine months. Every time we got wounded soldiers, my husband used to check them. If they were serious, he would put them in the Fiat car, take them down to the hospice, and do open anesthesia. Imagine, under shelling of bombs he was the one responsible to give open-air ether.[4]

The late Doctor Ibrahim Tleel was doing the surgery. Dr. Tleel was an excellent surgeon and very dedicated. He may have been the only remaining surgeon. I can't remember who else was there at the time. There wasn't an Augusta Victoria Hospital. There wasn't a Makassed Hospital. There was nothing. Only us.

I remember very well, whenever he went down to the Old City to give this open ether, Mother Martha used to tell him, "Get some bread, some this, some that," and she never went to sleep until my husband came back. He would see her, as he came in his Fiat car to this big iron gate, sitting on the terrace, waiting, worrying whether he would come back alive or dead, because they were shooting to separate Jerusalem from Bethany.

What a beginning for a marriage that was still intact, both partners alive and loving each other, after fifty years! In those early days of their marriage, Amin's career involved Betty, and their medical training came into full play. Amin continued to do many other civic tasks in the same good-natured spirit he employed as a professional healer of children:

He was a municipal councilor in Jerusalem for sixteen years and deputy mayor for one year. During the British Mandate, they used to take turns—one a Christian, one a Jew—but then when we were under Jordan, they changed this, and the mayor was always Moslem. Then they had elections: two city councilors from the Greek Orthodox, one from the Latin. Then they changed that rule, and everybody was free to run for election, and whoever won would get to be a city councilor.

I remember very well one of our dear friends who always was a councilor from our congregation came to my husband and said, "I hear you are running for election. Why don't you withdraw and just give me the chance?"

Amin said, "No, we're doing this the democratic way. Whoever loses will come and congratulate the winner." And so they ran for election, and my husband was the only Christian who won the election and became the only municipal councilor. Later he was asked to be acting mayor for one year when Mayor Rouhi Al Khatib had to go abroad in 1957. And he has been acting mayor [for East Jerusalem] from that time until now.

Long before the Oslo Accords were signed in 1993 the Arabs were developing a shadow government for their dreamed-of Palestinian state.[5] In the midst of them was the beloved shadow mayor of Jerusalem, Amin Majaj.

Betty's daughter Randa speaks fondly of the twenty-six years her mother spent at home rearing her family. Remarkably, her father's political career did not interfere with her perfectly normal childhood:

Mom was a real housewife. She was home when we finished our day at school. We always had a good meal after school. She was a wonderful cook, and we usually helped in the kitchen. We never had house chores as American children do.

Most summer vacations we spent in Beirut with our grandparents. Majdalouna was the village where they lived up in the hills. It was long before the war, and everything was beautiful.

We went to the beach at the American University of Beirut because my mom was an alumnus and it was a good, safe beach.

We had birthday parties that were a big deal. Every Sunday morning we'd go to church. Sunday was our family day. Some Sundays in winter we went to Jericho, and the children rented bicycles and rode around. We took ballet classes, and once a year we had a recital. Our teacher was Russian and French. She was excellent and spoke only French and very little Arabic. We all had music lessons—even my mom took piano when we were learning from a teacher who came to our home. Our family life was all-important to my parents.

Betty's obvious love for Amin and her four children and three grandchildren confirms that her family was her first concern. She often speaks of wanting to be a "proper wife." She is always looking for the correct balance between family and career, once her children were grown. "That balance often comes at the cost of your own nerve endings," she says.

We must fill our husband's needs—cup and spoon and everything. When a woman has a family, she is needed. The mother is needed. When the time comes that she can really cope—when the children are on their own—then she can choose to work. But then, it is not always the woman's choice whether she works or not.

I was always there as the children returned from school. I could easily imagine the frustration of a child who rushed home with problems and no mother to tell. It is in the family that the culture is built. It is the mother who does the building.

Betty worked as nursing matron of Augusta Victoria Hospital for ten years. Then she stayed home to be with her children and to rear them for the following twenty-five years. Her work as director of Princess Basma Center filled the next fifteen years. That work has been complicated as she seeks to fill the needs of poor Arab families of the West Bank, whose disabled children have to cross Israeli checkpoints to get to their treatment. Permits have become her nemesis.

Politics have been part of her life from the moment she came to live in Jerusalem in 1948 just after a new state had been born. The more than fifty years since then have added to a bureaucracy and to Betty's patience at every turn. How many, many times she has exclaimed as we talked, "What can you do?" The rhetorical question can only be answered by the wholly unsatisfying notion, "Wait." Nevertheless, she is constantly looking forward.

Her vision of the future of the Princess Basma Center includes a vocational training program for physically disabled young adults in East Jerusalem. She hopes to continue the pioneering efforts of integrating able-bodied and disabled children in school. While the peace process starts and stops and starts again, she goes on upgrading the services and training those who render them at the Center. Her continuing interest in linking to other local and international medical institutions crosses traditional political lines.

Not far from the center she now directs, Betty Majaj began her career as a nurse, assisting her new husband in Jerusalem. What a circle of caring she has nurtured for more than fifty years! What informed experience she brings to the task!

Her great disappointment in all her years in Jerusalem has been the recent years of conflict with so little resolved after hopes have been so high for peace. Yet she remains optimistic:

There will always be people against the peace process, but this period of time is a test for those people who are for it, to prove that it can work. It takes time to develop mutual confidence and trust. Fear has played a big part in it—doubt, fear, and lack of mutual respect. We can't harass each other, humiliate each other, and expect friendship to happen.

There are times, usually after a bomb kills innocent families in a market or on a busy street, when the spotlight focuses on the Middle

East. Have the reporters helped or hindered our understanding of the situation?[6] Have the media brought harm or good? Betty answers:

> They can do either harm or good. If you hear the news here in English it's different than in French; it's different in Hebrew, it's different in Arabic. So they play on each one's mind and mentality. And we were taught never to believe what you read or what you hear because it is tailored for public consumption.
>
> The media act as if it is a sin to change your mind. Yet a Prime Minister is asked the moment a story breaks what he thinks. There is nothing wrong with changing your mind if you believe you have made a mistake or after you've had time to analyze the situation or have been given more information. Then it deserves a different solution—a different approach.

Betty's analysis of the situation of Israeli settlers who have come from all over the world is perceptive. They come anticipating their own vine and fig tree and a secure existence, their high hopes matching hers when she came as a bride.

> These are settlers that the government brought over—uprooted them from all over the world and put them on the land and told them. "This is your land. Dig it up, live on it and use it." Then they come and tell them, "You have to leave and go somewhere else, because we cannot have peace without trading your land for peace." The settlers are not to blame if they act the way they do. Some of them are extreme. They can't just be told, "We're giving up the Golan for you." Slowly, they must get their minds ready, slowly, slowly, slowly.[7]

What a levelheaded attitude, willing to try to understand the views of others, not just crying out to be understood!

Can a diverse population share a land? That is the age-old question. Peoples across the earth are answering with their own battles over boundaries; Jerusalem and Israel are far from unique. Betty speaks of this, too:

This land is for everybody. Let's share it together. Our fate is to live together—Christians, Muslims, Jews. Both sides have had so many lost opportunities.

Her words made me think of Anna Grace Lind. Betty had known Bertha Spafford Vester and Anna Grace since she first came to Jerusalem. We spoke of them.

I have a painting that Bertha gave me. When I came as a bride, Bertha used to ask us, some women of Jerusalem, to go attend sewing sessions. She had weekly sewing sessions for the poor, and we used to have bazaars with whatever we sewed and sell them and the proceeds went to the poor. Every time I go to the American Colony I can't help but remember. When you go into the courtyard, the first room on the right—you go right up two steps—that was the sewing room for us. I wasn't very good, but she always found something for me to do. Her sister, Mrs. Whiting used to do the most interesting Christmas cards out of old used stamps. I had one, and I was so sorry that I lost it. Mrs. Vester was a very strong personality. Mrs. Whiting was on the quiet side, always doing what she had to do on the quiet and never daring to outshine Mrs. Vester.

Betty told me an interesting tale, a rumor, of how the two Spafford sisters had come to be married in the American Colony community. She had heard that the community did not intend for anyone to marry.

Anna Spafford, it was said, dreamed a dream in which she learned that her daughter Bertha was to marry Frederick Vester, the son of German missionaries in Jerusalem.

This is how she got her first daughter married. Then she dreamed another dream. This is not in her book, but we knew from our mother-in-law that she had another dream that her other daughter must get married to Mr. Whiting.

Mr. Whiting was my husband's patient. In the '40s and '50s there were no doctors there. Very few had come back, and very few had remained. Even though they were told that Amin was a pediatrician, they said, "No, you must come and treat him." He used to have a meal with him every day. He was in bed with TB and severe asthma. There was a new medicine and Amin used it on him. Mr. Whiting improved, and he was very grateful.

The network of Jerusalem in these years included Christian, Jew, and Muslim. Again I was surprised to see the interaction among the families of the women I was meeting. But at the time I didn't realize how much like a small town Jerusalem could be. Of course, the fact that there were few doctors meant they were called on to treat a wide range of patients. Still, I was amazed at the crossovers that kept cropping up. I expected that Betty would know Mary Franji—and she did, but it was not from the nursing profession, which they had in common. Betty had known Mary as an almost adopted daughter to Bertha Spafford Vester:

Mary knows about all these things because she lived with them [the Vesters]. I talked with her when she was young [in 1948, Mary was twenty-four and Betty twenty-one]. I remember how they married her to Mr. Franji, and she stayed with them until today, outliving them all. I'm glad that they [the Vesters] made it easier for her to marry this Arab who was much older but from a good family.

My curiosity piqued, I asked Betty about Anna Grace Lind, realizing that their time in Jerusalem had also overlapped.

Someone told me after Anna Grace died that my family's picture was on the mantel at Anna Grace's home when they went to dress the body. I said, "Our family?" She said, "Yes, you, your husband and the children."

Then I remembered that the last few years Anna Grace was so disappointed every time she came to church. I would greet her and talk to her and it brought back memories of the old days, the good old days, and all that.

Once she told me, "Betty, you know I'm very grateful. You're one person who stops and talks to me from all the congregation." I told her, "They're younger people here who don't know you. I'll never forget how much I admired you every time you parked in front of our house, when you were out driving your car."

Very few ladies drove cars at the time. Her posture driving the car with her hands in these white gloves was something to see. It was quite a sight. She was so chic with her white blouse and her hat. She was a very attractive woman.

Both Betty and Anna Grace were attractive when I knew them as mature women. I pictured them in my mind as women in their thirties or forties with the same energy and drive but with younger bodies and the stamina to rush around Jerusalem doing good. Picturing them in church together was inspiring.

Betty knew Hind Husseini, too, and saw her as larger than life, a real heroine:

The Husseini family are the aristocracy of the Muslim community, and they all have mansions. You know the Orient House was a Husseini house. Hind sort of bought up [property from] everybody she could in her family to establish her school, Dar El Tifl. We heard she went to Saudi and she raised five million [dollars].

Betty compared Hind Husseini and Bertha Spafford Vester: They were both "royal," but Hind said little and "her work talks for her."

Betty's work speaks for her, too. She has made a career of helping those who suffer; healing has been her vocation. She is sensitive to suffering, believing that those who have suffered should have developed compassion for those who presently suffer. She can't understand how we can recognize suffering in individuals but miss it on the larger scale of nations.

Her own philosophy of life is centered in service. She seems to be constantly asking, "Why are we even here if we can't help each other?" She began her career as a nurse on the Mount of Olives in 1948 when her husband went to fetch her from Beirut to help him operate a makeshift hospital in Jerusalem. Although ill herself, she answered him simply, "We will go back."

During the war in 1967, she refused to leave Jerusalem. Today, she keeps the Princess Basma Center going, and, until his death in 1998, she tended her ailing husband in that same home with the bullet hole still in the front door. After having celebrated her fiftieth wedding anniversary, she was still the pioneer bride who arrived in Jerusalem in 1948, giving of herself daily and refusing to count the cost: "filling her husband's needs—cup and spoon and everything."

Another friend of mine, Sandra Rogers, also a nurse, paid tribute to such women as Betty Dagher Majaj: "What marvelous principles those early pioneers teach us: to plant the best of seeds, without concern for praise or glory, to contribute something to the lives of people we may never see again!"

Notes

1. The Zionist movement dates to Theodore Herzl, who in Europe in 1896 urged the formation of a Jewish state in Palestine and the return of the Jews to that place, their Zion.

2. While Israelis fight to keep their hope in the future alive, they remain in control of Jerusalem, though that is far from an easy task. Long-time mayor Teddy Kollek held the view that there should be One Jerusalem, meaning a city that was home to a diversity of people ethnically and religiously but who were one as citizens of

Jerusalem. He worked throughout his twenty-six years as mayor to maintain a city open to all who came to it. He had running battles with the ultra-orthodox Jews, but his successor courted them. They helped elect him and then went to him for favors. The kind of balance for which Mayor Kollek was famous and even admired by the Palestinians has now flip-flopped. The present mayor has allowed Jewish housing to be built in areas of Jerusalem traditionally felt by Palestinians to be their domain. The line in the sand is moving, and the Palestinians fear for the future. For that matter, so do the Israelis, as the peace process falters and trust dwindles. On the Palestinian side, discouragement is palpable.

3. *Dunam* is a unit of land area used especially in the state of Israel. It is equal to one thousand meters or a quarter of an acre.

4. "Open-air ether" meant to drip very flammable ether, an anesthetic used to put a patient to sleep, onto gauze placed on a strainer over the patient's nose. Carrying out this procedure with bombs and fires all around would have been a terrible risk.

5. The Oslo Accords set ground rules for the Madrid Peace Conference.

6. "Reporter" is an interesting term for those who sometimes tell us not what has happened but how we are to think about it. Their presentations can color and blur the picture for those who cannot be eyewitnesses but depend upon television networks to bring the world into their living rooms.

7. It is interesting that in Hebrew, *Li'at, li'at, li'at* means "slowly, slowly, slowly." Both Arabic-speaking and Hebrew-speaking people use this colloquialism.

8. VERA RONNEN

We were quite assimilated Hungarians and didn't think that anything could happen to us [in World War II]—my father was an officer in the Austro-Hungarian army. Then, when the Germans invaded Hungary they started gathering [Jews]. It was luck for us that Hungary was the last country that they got to. We were picked up in our home and taken to a ghetto. Each city had a ghetto, you know, mostly disused factories or brick factories because the sheds that you dry the bricks in are very convenient to put up people. It was really a place to select people to send them off to various parts of the world and in Germany.

Vera Bischitz Ronnen

Vera Bischitz Ronnen is an appealing will-o-the-wisp—soft-spoken, gentle, and kind—with the bearing of a countess. Now in her mid-sixties, she is a loving, devoted mother and grandmother. Corners of her beautifully appointed homes in London and Jerusalem are stocked with children's treasures, and her larder is filled with sweets and fruits she knows they like.

One never would have guessed that she had known personally the horrors of the Holocaust. Although we talked of many things, until the day of our formal interview she never spoke to me of that part of her history. An account in the *Jerusalem Post* gave me general information: "The holocaust decimated Hungary's Jews, wiping out more than 600,000 men, women and children. The Germans did not occupy Hungary until 1944, and their late entry may have contributed to the ferocity of their extermination campaign. Many were deported to Auschwitz, and many more died in forced labor camps. The remaining Jews of Budapest were rounded up in late 1944, gathered on bridges over the Danube, and shot dead into the water."[1]

Miraculously, Vera Bischitz and her family were spared.

I first met Vera at a small dinner party given by mutual friends in Jerusalem. We were seated beside each other and conversed easily. Before the evening ended, our friendship had begun.

This attractive woman is an accomplished artist-teacher whose work is prominently displayed in Israel and in major cities of the world. Her enamels cover whole walls and are fired in a gigantic kiln. Some practice the art of enamelware on small objects like jewelry. Not Vera. She thinks in large scale, and she creates in large scale, in bright bands of color. One of her pieces, commissioned by American Express in Moscow, is a freestanding screen six and a half feet high. She spends much of her time teaching the craft she has mastered to others at the renowned Bezalel Art Institute of Hebrew University in Jerusalem.

Her home in Jerusalem, situated behind green gates on the Street of the Prophets, straddles east and west Jerusalem and is almost within sight of the Old City walls. It is encircled by a colorful garden shaded by large, old trees. She often rues the fact that she hasn't spent

Vera and her grandson

enough time in pruning and trimming, but the tangle of greenery and flowers is magical—a secret garden. It reflects the occasional gardener and is the perfect setting for the gracious, 150-year-old stone house with its high ceilings and arches.

It once was the home of the Anglican Bishop of Jerusalem and sported stables and tennis courts. Now it nestles among the trees and other greenery, a benevolent reminder of an earlier era in this ancient city. I am certain it was never more tastefully decorated than it is now. It is one of my favorite spots in all Jerusalem.

On the day of our interview, Vera was tending her newborn grandson while the baby's mother, Vera's younger daughter Keren, fulfilled a contract that would further her career in textile design. Vera had made a three-month commitment to help in this way, putting aside her own concerns for the moment. The tiny baby boy punctuated our exchange with little newborn noises, seeming to enjoy our dialogue nearly as much as we two grandmothers enjoyed the baby patter.

Vera begins:

I was born in [a part of] Hungary [that] became Romania and then Hungary again and is Romania now. I started in a Romanian school, but Hungarian is my mother tongue. My parents spoke Hungarian.

After being "gathered" by the Germans as World War II was winding down, Vera and her family were taken from the ghetto in Cluj, their own city, to a camp in Budapest where further selecting went on. From there they were shipped to the Bergen-Belsen concentration camp. Miraculously Vera was not separated from her father, mother, brother and grandmother during this time.

We were in Bergen-Belsen several months and luckily—I mean, it was a miracle—a Hungarian man called Kastner tried to make a deal with the Germans for the remaining Jews still alive, to exchange them for spare parts because the Germans needed equipment, cars, and spare parts. So we were kept as hostages while the dealing was going on. He saved two thousand people, and we were among the two thousand.

She knew Kastner, she tells me, because he was from the same city as she. She explains that he was a well-known figure and a controversial one:

Not everyone can think of striking deals with the Germans. You have to be an unconventional person for that. There were others like him. There was a Schindler that you may have heard of. There were several.

She comments:

We stayed alive. We lived under terrible, terrible conditions and we were hungry, but because of this deal we were lucky that they just allowed us to survive.

She quickly adds that this was not the worst of the camps. There were degrees of degradation in the camps, and in Bergen-Belsen at this time, the women were separated from the men, but at least families were confined in the same camp.

We knew that my brother and father were there. We were all finally freed during the war and taken by those famous carts running back and forth, back and forth, the ones used because all the rails and the railway stations were so badly bombed.

Finally we arrived in Switzerland with the Red Cross. The Swiss were very reluctant to let trainloads of refugees in, and as you know, they had to turn some back. But they were very good to us. My parents were sent to an internment camp in a mountain place called Engleberg. You know those ski resorts were totally neglected and disused because of the war, and there were those huge, unheated hotels. They used to put the refugees in there.

The children were handed out to families with foster parents because they wanted the children to go back to normal life and to go to school. It was very hard, very difficult, to part with parents because during the war, in the camps, one shared absolutely everything, and one knew it was life or death. So suddenly to become a child again was quite a strain that was very difficult and very sad. There I was.

Much was left unsaid about specific experiences, but her "There I was" spoke volumes.

Vera went first to a foster family in Geneva, but that wasn't successful. Here was a Jewish teenager, a refugee, being shuffled from place to place without her parents. In Geneva she had to learn French "overnight":

I did not lose any time. You [had experienced] so much in the perils of life that you weren't a child. You weren't going to be held back a year in order to learn the language spoken. You were just supposed to get it over with. That wasn't a success.

I was under the auspices of the Red Cross, so the wonderful woman who was in charge of me decided that I would be better off in a school, not with a family. I was put in a monastery with nuns in Geneva. I was the only Jewish child there, so that wasn't a great success either. I was so much the odd one out that it was miserable.

Then they moved me to an Orthodox Jewish girls' school, which was much worse. There I was the goy [Gentile]. There I was the non-religious one. That was very bad, but I was in each of them for a bit.

Then, luckily, this very kind Swiss family from Zurich, a Jewish family with three children, got in touch with my parents [looking for word of their relatives]. They had some family members in our part of the world. When they heard about my existence, they said they would take me for one year. I went to live with them in Zurich, and I started going to school. Of course that was a change of language from French to German, but I knew German from home. In those days the Swiss would speak the dialect to make a clear statement about being different from the German Germans.

I was there for a year exactly. On the dot of the year they said, "All right, this is it. We took you for a year."[2]

How did this child who had been wrenched away from her childhood meet this ultimatum?

It came time for me to choose a profession. I was not quite sixteen. I was in touch with my parents, but they were still in the internment camp with no money. Through the kindness of the wonderful woman in the Red Cross who had taken an interest in me earlier—she agreed that I would [get to try] going to an art school. Of course it was an outrageous thing to do then for a refugee who needed to earn a living instantly. I should instead become a hairdresser or seamstress, and after a few months training I would be ready to start working. My father was also quite upset about it, because I was being so impractical. We, of course, thought that we would go back to Hungary and be wealthy again, which certainly didn't happen.

But the Red Cross had a generous agreement that I would pay back whatever I was costing them after the war—after you started earning, you started paying back, which I did. They said, although it was a four- or five-year study, they would only finance the first one. So, again, my life was to be measured by one year. By then, if I was not able to get a grant, then it was my problem.

Typically, Vera didn't hesitate to launch into the four- or five-year program with the financing assured for only the first year. She believes that the "impossible" really *can* happen. She was able to maintain her own strong vision of herself in developing the talents she possessed. Perhaps such belief comes naturally to the young, or to the truly talented.

I went to Geneva, all on my own, and I found a little room.

For a while I lived in tiny little rented rooms. Then through incredible good fortune, through a very dear friend of mine, a classmate, I was able to rent a little old dilapidated apartment in the old city. The refugees were not allowed to rent unfurnished apartments. They were only able to rent second rentals. So her family agreed to do it for me under their name, and I had this very cheap, wonderful little apartment where the bathtub was in the kitchen and a little tree on the landing. It was great! It was absolutely wonderful.

I started my studies at the Beaux Art in Geneva, Switzerland. And I worked!

Her enthusiasm over her own tiny apartment lights up her eyes. What a giant leap from Bergen-Belsen to a "bathtub in the kitchen and a tree on the landing."

Her studies went on apace, and she won a grant to continue after the first year. She called herself lucky, but her subsequent success cannot be called luck.

The time came when I was to choose a specialized subject, and I wanted to become an architect but the architectural studies were very, very long. I remember the dean saying to me, "Why don't you just go look around to find something a little shorter? This one is so difficult, and it is so long, and it is so hard to find work."

So I went from department to department, and they let me sit in for a week in each department. I was fascinated by enamel, so that was it.

I've done that ever since. I stayed in Switzerland for five more years until 1950. In the meantime, my parents emigrated to Israel, and so did my brother, who joined the army.

That older brother, George, now lives in Los Angeles. He is her only sibling.

I haven't been too good at worrying about the future. When I wake up and start thinking early in the morning, my main concern is the health and well-being of my children and grandchildren.

I don't have a lifetime goal. If it was up to me, then I'd say that I'd like to do what I'm doing right now. Taking over the baby for three months totally is something that I've decided to do for Keren so that she can get on with her career.

What were the circumstances that first brought her to Jerusalem? After her years in beautiful Switzerland, it amazed me that she hadn't chosen to make her home in Europe. Israel would have been a backwater for an artist, not to mention the real hardships that existed during the time when she chose to come.

The answer is—she fell in love.

I came to Jerusalem on a visit first, to see my parents. Through my brother, George [who lived in Israel then], I met my first hus-

*band, he was a friend of his. We fell in love, got engaged, and I
went back to finish my studies. Then I came to live here. We lived
in the house next door.*

And so, at twenty years of age, Vera was married. It is astonishing
to look back at her life experiences up to this point and realize that
she was only twenty years old and starting married life.

*I started working at Bezalel Academy instantly and met the then-
director of the Bezalel art school. It wasn't an academy yet. He
was called Ardon, and he was a very famous Israeli painter who
died recently. His name then was Bornstein, but he changed it to
Ardon, and he was one of the well-known painters in the country. He said that I was the person he had been waiting for. They
had some equipment, a kiln, some colors, and plenty of room.*

   *I have to laugh because now, of course, there is never room
for a class or for another student. Then, I could just choose which
room would be suitable. I started teaching instantly. It was a very
difficult thing because I didn't speak Hebrew and I spoke very little English.*

But Vera spoke to me in impeccable English, learned at home with
her Australian husband. Her broad vocabulary is sprinkled liberally
with French and Hebrew phrases—and her Hebrew is also fluent.

*My English was not impeccable, but it was bearable. My Hebrew
is not as good as it could be. I speak it well, but my reading and
writing are poor because I never went to an Ulpan [Hebrew language school]. I didn't have time. I started teaching instantly,
and I became pregnant soon. So I taught and was exhausted
every day when I finished my teaching because I was in and out
of four or five languages, you know. Each student teaches you
another language.*

   *Then I had my daughter Michal. What a joy and delight she
is in my life these days! We are real friends, the kind who share*

everything. Our family moved over to this house, and I've never lived anywhere else for forty-five years. It was my first house since the Holocaust. It is very much my home, my first home, and my roots go very deep. I've never lived anywhere else.

After Michal was born, Vera continued teaching and working. She worked in small scale on her Swiss equipment, doing a lot of very classic enamel jewelry. Much of her time was spent in bringing up Michal. Then her second daughter, Keren, was born, and the family moved for a year and a half to South Africa when her husband was sent there by the government to work.

In South Africa Vera experienced an entirely different culture, and the experience broadened her artistic horizon. She began to think "big."

We came back, and I started working in a larger scale. When in South Africa, I was asked to do some panels, slightly larger than a piece of jewelry, and some door handles for a cinema. When I did that, an architect from Switzerland saw them and commissioned me to do something also for a cinema, and after that he saw my paintings and liked them a lot and wanted to know if I could do the elevator doors of his office building. That was my first large commission, and I had absolutely no idea how to go about it, but I said yes.

The experiences of her early life came into play. Doing the undoable had been her training. Her confidence carried her along. It never occurred to her that a thing couldn't be done.

This must have been in 1963, or 1964. [She was then thirty-three or thirty-four.] One thing led to another. I did those elevator doors by renting a little corner in a factory in Basel. I found a place, and I started commuting a lot between Switzerland and here and working terribly hard under a lot of pressure. I had a very good assistant who stayed in Switzerland and would make

all the preparations for me when I'd come, and then we'd work
around the clock.

After agreeing to her first large commission, Vera found her
career skyrocketing as her hard work paid off. She received plaudits
for finished pieces and commissions to produce new projects.

I won competitions, I got marvelous commissions from the chem-
ical industry in Basel, and I did some huge murals. I had a tem-
porary studio put up next to the factory because when I started
working so much they wouldn't have me inside. So they put up
one of those prefabs that you have on building sites with a con-
necting corridor and I used to work there. I rented the land from
a peasant who usually planted potatoes there. I paid him for his
potatoes plus, and he was delighted not to have to work. I had a
two-year agreement with him, and I stayed for fifteen years.

The entire family would go for the summer to Switzerland where
Vera would work and they would holiday. She explained that it was
very difficult for the family because often there was nobody there
they knew. She would be busy doing her work and meeting a stress-
ful schedule while the family waited.

The strain began to show in her marriage. She grew and developed as an artist and became confident and independent, but her
marriage atrophied and died.

Financially I was independent. I was no longer totally dependent
on my husband, which is a very difficult thing anyhow. He was a
kind person, but it was difficult. I also didn't have to borrow from
my parents anymore. I could pay them back whatever they had
lent us. It was a good feeling. The whole family benefited finan-
cially from my working because I could spend for a car and a
washing machine, and all those little things that matter so much.
The one thing that we didn't do, because I never had the urge of
ownership, was to purchase our house.

I've learned my lesson and what it means is that you own so much and you lose it in a minute. If I had thought about that I would have tried to buy this place where I am now.

I still keep an eighteenth-century studio in London in sight of the Thames river.

So, I ask, is she London-based or Jerusalem-based? She seems to feel no confusion on this point. Jerusalem is home. Her London studio symbolizes her craft, her art, and her profession.

I would not like to feel that I'm living here in Jerusalem one hundred percent. As a woman on her own, I don't want to give up my studio in London. If I came back to live here year round, it would be a little like a semi-retirement. Being in the cold of [England], fending for myself, keeps me on my toes.

I also have this working relationship; I have the factory nearby where I can use the huge kilns. So the setup is very good, and all I have to do is get a commission, and I know that within a few weeks I can have an exact answer from the factory—when it can be done, or how much it costs—and I can gear myself towards that.

Is London, then, the place to work, and Jerusalem the place to rest, play, be with family?

Some parameters begin to emerge as Vera thinks through her reasons, her impulses. She sees her life as a kind of two-part harmony between the cold of England and the temperate warmth of Mediterranean life:

I have a circle of friends here in Jerusalem, but I have a different circle of friends in London. Very different. Here they are more family-oriented. In London there are more professional single people who I have become friendly with through my work, but they are very independent people there. Of course, I have met others through mutual friends. But here in Jerusalem it is more of a community.

Her daughter Keren lives in Israel, and Michal spends much time in Israel through the year because her husband, a famous architect, has ongoing project and keeps an office there.

Both homes contribute to a basic order in Vera's life, which lends stability.

We speak of items in homes having places they belong. "That goes there, and this goes here," are phrases we often use. Vera speaks for every woman, I think, when she says:

Familiarity in your hometown or city is a comfort. Supermarkets where we know our way around; which aisle has the dairy products, etc. These things, the visual images which surround us, are woven into patterns like background music, which help us feel comfortable, lend us a certain comfort zone.

Here in Jerusalem, there is also a small-town feeling. I know many people, even shopkeepers. My life in London is different. There I fend for myself and feel more isolated.

It was almost surreal to be sitting there, speaking of high-powered people, exotic places, exhibitions, generous commissions, while this casually dressed grandmother cooed at her grandson, almost forgetting that I was there. In this setting it was easy to ask her directly about her art, her work. She is quick to respond:

It's essential. My work is essential. You know I don't want to sound like a workaholic, but I know that I structure my life around it. Suddenly the next thing is you are moaning because it is too much work, or the pressure is too great, or something, but that is good.

The work gives me a firm base from which I can function. I go to London and see exhibitions, and I visit places and meet people. I feel like I am stimulated to be a better artist. I find there are other things that I'd love to do. I have a lot to say, I have a lot to teach.

Vera, who is aging gracefully, speaks quite philosophically about the process:

I think that as we grow older we recognize that we are on the last leg of our lives. No matter how beautifully you put it, we are not in the youth of old age. There is this time limit.

I don't know how much more time there will be to work. When I think of it rationally, I just wonder how much time I still have to be doing those gigantic, difficult things.

Our conversation was interrupted by a sudden burst of birdsong from the garden, and we stopped for a moment to listen to the birds. When she spoke again, Vera said, "It is so quiet around here. There's nobody upstairs."

Her statement seemed to echo in the elegant room. She was quite alone in her beautifully designed space. Today the baby and I were there, both of us taking in the colorful environment. The bright and beautiful colors caught the infant's eye. The engaging chatter of his grandmother with her hugs and snuggles telegraphed to him her unbridled love. I, too, felt her kindness and warmth in allowing me into her life without pretense. I, too, drank in the beautiful setting, a feast for my eyes that would not have been complete without the tender image of the woman and child. Vera is indeed a consummate artist, but she is not only that. Both mothers and artists are givers without stint.

This picture of Vera Ronnen would be incomplete without a postscript from the year 2000. All the bright hope for her future of which we spoke and which seemed inevitable on that sunny day in her home came crashing down.

Her daughter Keren died, a gradual death drawn out through months of chemotherapy and the struggle to find a match for a bone marrow transplant. Vera mothered and cradled her dying child to the end. Then Keren was gone.

One rarely expects to outlive one's children. It is a gigantic blow to the heart. No one can really enter that sacred, solitary place to comfort. Yet time passes, and beloved grandchildren become more and more a part of Vera's life. She is quick to point out that roles reverse and the giver receives, the helping helps the helper. She has come to the time when she draws strength from the children and grandchildren to whom she always offered her strength. Indeed, she has never stopped offering it.

Such reservoirs of strength may be hidden in each of us. Sadly, we never know for sure until the test comes. Vera's devotion to her family has made peace possible beyond the boundaries of her own grief.

Notes

1. "From Budapest to Jerusalem," *Jerusalem Post,* January 15, 1996, Special Section, 18.
2. As fate would have it, Vera received a letter in 1995 from the kind woman at the Red Cross, Elizabeth Bertchi, who lives in Geneva, Switzerland.

9. SAHIR DAJANI

I am not a feminist. I wanted to act according to the village women's conservative culture and yet liberate them. Believe me, I have succeeded in that. When we began they were so shy they wouldn't look me in the eye. Now, they will even argue with me—and with men—stronger than I would!

Sahir Dajani

The lovely Palestinian woman stepped out of the remodeled house that served as a shop for traditional Palestinian embroidery to have her photo taken in the garden among the roses. She came reluctantly, and I quickly snapped a couple of photos in the bright Jerusalem sunlight. Conservative Muslims sometimes worry that photographs invite the Evil Eye, but this notion didn't trouble Sahir. She was simply modest and surprised that anyone would want her picture.

I had seen Sahir in the showroom on other occasions, and we had always chatted pleasantly, but this time I asked her name. Sahir explained that she was in charge of the embroidery project that produced the lovely items lining the walls of the shop. She told me enthusiastically how poor Palestinian women in the towns south of Jerusalem produced traditional cross-stitch designs from their villages on various items to sell to tourists. The Mennonites sponsored and managed the program, seeing to the distribution of quality materials and the marketing of the finished products in the city.

Each time I returned to Jerusalem during the next ten or twelve years, I stopped by the showroom. I loved the authentic Middle Eastern embroidery. What I had learned from Sahir years earlier helped me to feel supportive of the project—and also aroused my curiosity. I knew intuitively that Sahir had a remarkable story to tell. We visited a little more each time we met, and over time we became friends.

I found that she had been closely associated with Hind Husseini, and had taken Hind as a role model when she was young. Both women had been involved in the Palestinian community of Jerusalem. But I was surprised to learn that Sahir, as a young mother, had taken her children to the Spafford Center for care, and there she knew the Vesters and Anna Grace Lind.

Such an intermingling of lives in Jerusalem is not unlike small-town America. On first meeting each of these women, I had no idea that they knew each other, yet I found that their lives intersected, some of them deeply.

Sahir Dajani's family had been in Jerusalem for eight hundred years. She was born on December 9, 1940, in Ashkelon, on the coast of the Mediterranean Sea south of Tel Aviv and Jaffa.

I'm a Muslim by birth. But we are not very conservative Muslims. We were brought up in nun's school. [She laughs.] I was very young when I finished high school, about sixteen. I went just one semester to the American University in Cairo. After that I came back home and got married. I wasn't yet eighteen when I got married.

It was an arranged marriage. When I came back home many people came to visit us. Then one of these came to ask for my hand. This is the word for it. My father asked me whether I agreed, whether I approved of this engagement. He even told me, "If you want to go back to college, I'm happy to send you back to college, and if you want to get married, fine."

Our tradition says that at a certain age a woman should get married, so I decided that I wanted to get married. [The man who had asked for Sahir's hand came to her home.] I have a British sister-in-law, so I asked her when he came, "Why don't you talk to him and find out if he's conservative, and if I can live with him. Just examine this man before I decide." My sister-in-law sat with him, he spoke good English, and she said, "Sahir, he's very, very good. He's not conservative. I'm sure you will live fine with him. He's a good man." So I said fine. I agreed. He's about ten years older than I am. When we had the engagement, I asked my parents to put a condition that I would like to finish my university work after we got married. So they told him that. He said fine. There is no written contract with regards to these things; it is just verbal.[1]

Sahir spoke shyly of the intricacies of an arranged marriage, including the sleuthing she had requested by one she trusted to help her make the decision. Her culture had prepared her for such a choice. This was not an isolated young woman, trying to make up her mind alone. There was comfort in knowing her father and mother and other relatives had a deep interest in her future happiness. Even an American girl growing up at the same time would have had considerable input from her parents in choosing a marriage partner.

There were unspoken as well as spoken requirements, both religious and social. These customs might have changed radically in America, but not in Jerusalem. The culture still requires that certain traditional conditions be met before a marriage may be solemnized, and those conditions were met before Sahir was married.

> *So I got married, in 1959, and I lived for many years as a wife and mother, without working outside of my home. We went to the States; I did not have the chance to go to the university then.*
>
> *My husband, however, graduated from Utah State University in Logan, Utah. He did some undergraduate work and also his graduate work there. We lived in Logan two years. Palestinian families are very close to each other, very much like the Mormons we met, with some of the same kinds of family traditions. We had a very good time in Utah among the Mormons. Some of the best years I have spent were in Utah. I had a boy who was born there and returned to school, to his birthplace, for one year but the winter was too cold so he moved to California. [She laughs.]*
>
> *My husband, Shehadeh, was really liberated and very open-minded, and we lived happily. I was young, I did not know many things about life! He's the only boy from his family with two other sisters. It's not an easy thing for a woman to get married to an only son. I faced many things in my life, but I tried to overcome all these at that young age.*

How tenderly she characterized this early period of her married life. The understatement with which she recalled the challenges of being married to an only son showed respect and restraint, perhaps gained over time. Her youthful stamina helped her to meet challenges in her early married years with verve and energy. That same youthful enthusiasm is part of the mature woman who now exhibits such grace and dignity. She loved her family and cared for them as completely as any woman could. But the unwritten contract that provided for her to finish her education was not forgotten.

Then when the time came, in 1973, I said to myself and then to my husband that I wanted to go back to the university. This was after I had my four children. He said, "If you want to go back, that's fine." I was interviewed, and they said, "You can come back to the university." So I went to Birzeit University, in Ramallah. It wasn't easy with four children. My husband helped me a lot.

I sent my little boy to the nursery at the Anglican school. It was very good, and we managed. It was a challenge for a Palestinian woman to go to the university, along with all the other duties of cooking, cleaning, and all these home things. It was something unusual. I had no hired help in my home.

Any woman anywhere in the world who takes seriously the rearing of her children is stretched thin to keep everything going in her household while she studies at a university.

Our children went to private schools, and you know how much work they give them, whether it was St. George's or Schmidt's. I needed to help them with their homework. So I was doing that, but my husband was helping me. The most important thing was his being with the children in the afternoon whenever I was late at the university. This was a big help to me because if I knew that I had to leave my children alone, I would have sacrificed the university because I did not want to be away from them, especially in the afternoon. Shehadeh encouraged me in many, many ways.

Sahir finished her bachelor's degree in sociology with a teaching certificate. She graduated in only three years, having begun in 1973 and finishing in the summer of 1976. During the last semester she was at the university, a chance conversation began a chain of events that changed her life:

My husband had good contacts with the Mennonite Central Committee (MCC). Paul, the director of the Mennonite Central Committee, said, "Shehadeh, we want someone to manage the

Palestinian needlework program. An aggressive woman. A woman with a strong personality who can take over, because the Palestinian needlework program was run by an expatriate. So now we want to localize the project, and we need someone." So my husband said, "Sahir, if you know of a woman or a girl or someone who can take this job at the Mennonite Central Committee let me know." I said, "Well, I will ask and see, and if there is, I will tell you."

In the meantime, I went to the Mennonite Central Committee and applied for the job, without telling my husband at all. I knew that the director didn't know me because he had never met me. He had no idea that I was Shehadeh's wife. After a first interview and second interview with a few people he said, "Yes, we will take you."

Did she handle the matter this way to be certain that she got the job on her own merits and not in any way because of her husband? Or was she concerned that no matter how liberal Shehadeh was, he might not have been favorable to such an arrangement? Or was she merely moving to the next logical step as she finished her studies?

I was willing, at that point, to omit my last semester at the university in order to take this job. But when I found that they wanted me so badly, I said that I wanted to take this job but that I needed to finish the last semester. I said, "Paul, I will take the job, but I still have six credits to finish." He said, "Of course, we want you to finish the university. You will start working with us in February, but you'll go to the university and work here half-time or full-time, whatever you feel like doing. Whenever you want to come, you come to work, and then you go to the university."

They recognized her ability and capacity to do their work. She was, indeed, a strong woman and ready to apply her talents to their project.

The triple responsibilities of home plus work plus finishing university training left her out of breath but happy. She was very much aware of her young son but no longer wished to depend on her husband to be with him in the afternoons:

> I was leaving home at seven and going to work. Then at ten-thirty I had classes. I'd go to class to Birzeit University, come back to the MCC work, and then in the afternoon work a few hours.
>
> I had to make time for my little boy who was still young. I said, "I have a little boy." and he said, "You can bring him over to work with you. He can do his homework while you do your work."
>
> So that's what I did until I finished my semester and graduated. Then I was promoted. I got a salary, and my title was manager of the Palestinian Needlework Program. It wasn't an easy thing to work. It was a challenge because the project was a big one.

The Palestinian Needlework Project had been started in 1952 by the Mennonites. It was begun in Jericho as a small project with a few women. Later they moved to frontier villages in the south because that area was considered the most undeveloped in the West Bank. It still is.

> They worked in few villages in the south. At that time they did not have many girls working for the project, but when I worked with the project we had around six hundred women working in the different areas and the camps. To work in the project was not an easy thing for me, but from the beginning I felt there was an object in working with these women.

Sahir felt she had the power to change the circumstances of some of these women by working towards carefully determined objectives.

> It's not easy. You have to believe in the change yourself before you can impose it or apply it or work towards it. Once you believe, then you have a target. It is an objective then, and you work towards that objective. From my experience, once you have this

goal, then things would begin to happen. I saw this during my work and in my whole life, even raising my children. I felt this way on many levels, and I saw the changes take place at home, outside, or wherever I was.

Administering the needlework project was not a ploy to gain personal power. Sahir's work with the women of the villages was woman to woman. There was no power to be had in this setting. Palestinian women, including Sahir, traditionally have very little power in the usual sense. Their strength derives from the influence they have on their husbands, brothers or fathers. The men make informed political decisions, shaped by the women in their lives.

I wanted to work with what I considered the grass-roots women. Whether their people considered them grass-roots or not, I don't know. But for me, they were real people that should have a change. I worked with them, not only because I wanted to earn money, but there were other things that I wanted to work with them to accomplish. I wanted to help them change their lives, their social lives—the way things were running in their families, in the environment, in their villages. The way they looked at life.

This was no modest goal. Centuries of tradition would have to be challenged.

Women's roles had been well defined, and any move to change the status quo was viewed suspiciously by the women themselves and even more suspiciously by the men who lived with them and depended on them. In particular, the mukhtar, or chief, of each village or camp, needed to see the advantages of any project in his environs.

It was really a challenge for me, and I felt these were my target people, not those in the office in Jerusalem. I was directing seven employees in Jerusalem. But they were working there before I came, in this project. Some of them had more experience work-

ing with the project itself, but my main concern was the villagers themselves. I was spending maybe seven hours each day with them. I would leave at seven in the morning and not come back to the office until five.

She spent these ten-hour days in the villages. As manager of the project, she had to distribute embroidery materials to the village women. Fifty to one hundred women would arrive on the appointed day to be paid and to pick up more work to take home. The beautiful, traditional embroideries represented patterns known by heart in the areas she visited, patterns that might well be lost to coming generations if they were not practiced by these Palestinian women. I recalled Ulwiya Husseini and her deep desire to preserve her people's heritage "one stitch at a time."

I was managing the project. We had this work that was distributed to the different villages. But I was watching these women and talking to individual women about their problems, about their lives; any problems, any struggle that I found. Every day I would go and maybe sometimes even crying and the people would say, "What's going on, Sahir? Why are you upset today?"

I would answer, "I don't know, because there are so many things in the village that made me upset." You know, I wanted to change something but it wasn't easy for me from the first month or the first year to change anything.

This tenderness of heart in identifying with the women around her in such a profound way is characteristic of Sahir. Perhaps this would be true of most women, given the same circumstance. Sahir was watching and seeing. Women often see with different eyes than men do, and vice versa. That is probably good, particularly if men and women share what they see.

Maybe I was working as a social worker at the beginning, but at the same time I was gaining experience, trying to think what can

I do with this project. It's true it's helping the women to generate income, to help their family income, but how much is it helping them in the long run? Is it reaching the goal, our goal, my goal as a Palestinian? These questions were just in my mind.

I didn't change anything at first, because this was a project I had been hired to manage as it was planned and designed. But you see, I felt that the women were finding in me someone close that they can talk to. We talked about their husbands, their children, how do they go to school, whether they have enough to give their children, why their daughters are not going to school, why do they let them miss school.

There were so many women's issues that I was discussing with them and trying to help as much as I can. In many ways I was encouraging them, even, you know, trying to give them more work, trying to have more people get involved in the project. This continued from 1976 to 1985, I think.

It helped them in supplementing the family income in the villages. I don't know whether it raised their social life much, but it helped the women to do something while they were at home looking after their children and their husbands. The producers are the core of the whole project, and they were earning barely minimum. So I said, it's really a successful project, but it's not a healthy project. I concluded that I should find a way to change the whole structure of the project to raise the producers' incomes.

On the surface this sounds like a fine idea, one that any woman would be happy to adopt. But while Sahir's superiors were willing to look at other options, the producers themselves were worried. And those in management couldn't imagine anything that would work to change matters.

We want to do it as a viable commercial enterprise and be certain that the producers will benefit in the long run. Most of the income is not going directly to the producers. They said, "What do you suggest?" I suggested one thing, Transfer the project to the

*women producers—this is the only way. They said, "But how?" I
said, "It can work."*

*So, they said, "How can you trust the project to women who
know nothing about it? They do the work. They do the embroidery. They just give you the piece. They don't know beyond that."
I said, "No, we can orient them. We can train them about the
work."*

But Sahir had failed to anticipate her friends' reaction to this idea.
The village embroiderers thought they were being abandoned.

*I went to the villages. I went to the women. I gathered many of
them and I said, "Women, I'm thinking of one thing. To transfer
the project to you."*

They said, "What!?"

I said, "I want to give you the project. To run it yourself."

*They said, "Sahir, please be frank. Are you withdrawing?
Are you giving up on us? Are the Americans leaving?"*

*I said, "They are not leaving. They are staying here, but they
want to give you the project so you can benefit."*

The women couldn't believe it. They were afraid. This was a giant
unknown to them, and they had little enthusiasm for striding out
onto this uncharted path. Many of the women quit the project, and
some began to work in factories.

*They said, "No, we refuse this idea, and don't talk to us about it.
Please don't."*

*They were afraid. They said, "Do you think we can do what-
ever you are doing in Jerusalem? Do you think we can do the
management? Do you think we can do the accounting? Do you
think we can read the designs? Do you think we can cut, we can
inspect, we can hem?"*

I said, "Yes, you can!"

They said, "No, we can't. No way, Sahir."

*I said, "Yes. You can do the embroidery, which is more diffi-
cult than management, and you know accounting. I don't know
how to do embroidery, the cross-stitch." I said, "You can do it, so
you know more than I do."*

They said, "No."

*You know, after I said these words, many, many girls just quit
from the project, and they went to work in Israeli factories making bras and underwear in Bethlehem. When I went the second
time to the village I said, "Have you thought about the idea?"*

They were sure she was leaving the project, but she went to the
mukhtar and told him that the women were leaving the project
because she wanted to transfer the project to them. He said they did-
n't understand, so she said she wanted him to tell them to come back.
She had more ideas to convince them.

*Some of them came back, but not all of them. I said, fine. I
thought the best way was to take them to other projects in the
West Bank. Show them how other people are working. I took
them to another cooperative project where the women were doing
not only embroidery but helping in the production phases. So,
they were impressed with the idea of taking a little more responsibility but not the whole project.*

The process was a slow one, but Sahir's patient persistence was
effective. She asked for a list of the names of girls who would be interested in training. And she got a list of thirty women.

*I said, "Next time I want to bring for you equipment for train-
ing." So I purchased all equipment: tables, scissors, and
machines. Anything that has to do with the project—irons, ironing boards, ledger books. Everything!*

*I said, "I want names of girls who would like to be trained in
management, in accounting, in cutting, in hemming." I got
names for each of the different phases of production.*

Her people skills were remarkable, but this was not the result of training in organizational behavior. This was vintage Sahir, something that came with her at birth.

We started the training for all the villages in one village, Surif. Most of the training I did there, except for ironing, because they don't have electricity. I said, "Girls who want to be trained in ironing, we will take them over to our center in Jerusalem. We will pay them for their transportation. I will send the driver to pick them up on another day, and we will bring them over."

So we started training right away. The training took us one year, but they mastered all phases of production in less than one year. In six months, they did it all. So I said, "Now, you have mastered it, but we cannot duplicate the wage for a woman who is ironing in Jerusalem." In one year we started to transfer phase by phase. Gradually we transferred the whole process to the village women. Today it's the most successful cooperative on the West Bank.

Only Sahir's powers of persuasion brought the women to this point. They were reluctant retailers, willing to produce but frightened of taking the next step.

This is the last stage of our work. You see, once they learn how to do their own marketing, then we might withdraw. But the showroom is also for MCC. They might have another outlet, perhaps in Bethlehem, maybe in Hebron. But the Jerusalem MCC shop would remain open.

I was glad to hear that, because the city wouldn't be the same without it. The shop was wonderful, partly because of its location—away from the crowded, noisy streets of the Old City—and partly because of the lovely old house with its garden in the front. The same flowers had served as a background for the photographs of Sahir on that day nearly twenty years before.

Registering the cooperative was a huge task, and Sahir had her share of bureaucratic red tape to cut through. But after all that she had accomplished with the women themselves, she was not about to let that stop her.

I am still an advisor for them, a consultant. I remain part of the project. Whenever they need us for any advice, they come and we talk. Following the success of establishing the Surif Women's Cooperative, I was asked by the Jordanian Cooperative Organization in Jordan to establish similar women's cooperatives in the West Bank. My response was, "It is comparatively easy to gather women and then to register a cooperative, but to make it successful is the big question."

Having worked herself out of a job, Sahir moved into other ventures with women's groups where she could use the expertise she gained in the Surif project to help in the slowly evolving infrastructure of the Palestinian people.

After that I worked with the grass roots in income-generating projects. Not just traditional hand crafts but also with women organizations consulting for projects like food processing. They would approach MCC for technical assistance, or other times for financial assistance, for a certain project. Then I started to work mostly with economic development projects. Not only with women but with women and men. So any project that we get which is in need of development, whether it's agriculture, health, education, kindergarten, we try to help.

Sahir Dajani and her husband and children have lived in Jerusalem during most of their married life. From their present home in Shuafat, just north of Jerusalem, she travels over the tiny country within a country that hopes to one day be called Palestine.[2] She has a Jerusalem ID, so she can travel more easily than other Palestinians in the West Bank. Her four children are grown now, and the education she craved for herself when they were small has equipped her to serve in other important ways. She beams as she speaks of her family:

My daughter is now living in the States. She finished at Bethlehem University, in nursing, and earned a master's degree in child and family psychology in the States. She got married to a physician. It's a good thing for a doctor to be married to a nurse. They understand. He finished training in Canada and is presently working in the States.

Musa, the second son, who was born in Logan, Utah, graduated with an industrial engineering degree and is now a successful businessman in San Francisco.

The youngest is still going to school, working on his master's degree.

My oldest son, Hashem, is a surgeon. He's the one who's living in Shuafat not far from us. He joined St. Raphael Hospital in New Hamden, Connecticut, and received his American Medical Board in internal medicine.

We see Hashem's children, a boy and a girl, almost every day. We love them. We want them to stay with us all the time.

It is easy to see where Shehadeh has been through all of this. He kept his unwritten marriage agreement and supported his lovely wife in magnifying her talents in an extraordinary way. Besides that, he gathers his grandchildren in the evenings. His own work was always there to be done as well.

He used to work most of his life in Jerusalem and the West Bank, but now he's working in Jericho. He's the general director of the Arab Development Society. They run a dairy and a farm. The Mormons sent them the cows when Musa Alami started it.

He is a good man. My husband says, "God looks at what we do, how we think, and then He judges us. He doesn't judge you because you're a Muslim or a Christian." I agree with him.[3]

These shared values have governed Sahir's life. From that first day when I took her photo and realized she was not a conservative Muslim, I had sensed in her a deep commitment to God, but I wondered how she defined her religious belief.

> *You believe in the values of your religion. So you try to adapt it to your philosophy and whatever good you do. I begin with the good values of Islam. There are values in each religion. So you have to look at the good values and then live accordingly.*
>
> *But you also look at what is good in other religions. In Christianity, they forgive. Forgiveness is good! You realize that your religion does not have everything. You believe in forgiving, though you are not Christian. You just follow it because you try to do what's good and please God. You can seek good things from every place.*

Surely she had sought good from every source around her and had incorporated every idea she had discovered into her own philosophy. She spoke longingly of the luxury of peace.

> *Peace is the feeling that you are not threatened, that your children are not threatened and that your grandchildren might live in a peaceful environment. When you don't have to worry about your children going out, whether they will come back safe. This is the peace we seek.*

One of the most powerful influences on Sahir's life was Set Hind Husseini. She speaks of her with affection and admiration:

> *I knew her very, very well, because there is a tie between me and Hind Husseini. My mother is a Husseini. And because Hind was on the board of the Arab Development Society, she knew my husband very well.*
>
> *I visited her every once in a while because I admired her. She was really a great woman. She was a strong woman. And I don't*

think anybody can replace her. As busy as she was administering her school, she did her embroidery by her own hand and with her own designs.

Just a week before she died, I called Set Hind and talked to her.[4] Her mind was the same. She said, "Oh, Sahir, I haven't heard from you. Oh, why did you not come? Oh, I miss you."

"Tomorrow, tomorrow I will come to see you." So the next day I went to visit her.

She was in bed. She said, "How is your mother, you are my relative." And she started to tell me the history.

She said, "I'm proud of you, Sahir. I know what you do." Anyway, I said, "You know what? I went to the man who frames pictures, and I saw a piece of embroidery that [he is framing for you] that I liked so much."

She said, "I did it with my own hands, with pure silk threads."

I said, "Where did you get the pure silk threads?"

She said, "I just took it out from some cloth that was woven with silk."

I said, "I like it."

She said, "I'm happy to give you the pattern for it." So she asked her assistant, "Make a big picture for Sahir—a clear one so that I can give her this, because it's already framed, that one." She gave me a big picture. She wrote, "A present from Hind Husseini to my beloved Sahir." I still have it.

I loved her. She was a kind of a role model to me. She was strong. She was good, she had a big heart. She is respected.

I couldn't help saying, "You are so like her. I'm sure she's still pleased with what you do." Sahir replied:

I stick to things sometimes, though. I push hard. I am strong. I cope with the stress of my life by working hard. We put all our energy in our work. That's what I do. I want to do better and better, and maybe create other things that I can put all my stress

Sahir and Hidaya Husseini, Hind's adopted daughter

energy in, because this is the only outlet for me. We have to work more and more to prove ourselves that we are here in spite of everything, in spite of occupation, in spite of injustice, for we are a nation. We are a people.

No longer does Sahir spend seven hours a day traveling from village to village, from woman to woman, listening, helping those with feeble knees to higher ground. These days she works with economic development on a new scale. As cofounder of the Economic Development Group, a credit institution, she has her work cut out for her. Others may wait for outside sources to fund the needs of the Palestinians. Not Sahir. The last time we met, she was hurrying away to a meeting where the agenda was to merge several fledgling credit organizations into one.

I am on the committee that is following the merging of the three organizations. So I want to see, where did we get with the lawyer, with the registration, with the new legislation.

She had learned how to register a cooperative of women who embroidered. Her practical training taught her how to move from the grass roots up. She told me once that this is the only way such projects will ever succeed. It can't work from "up to down." She believes that, and so she operates from "down to up" and does it so effectively. She patiently changes things and is willing to do it gradually. I told her once, "Sahir, you could do anything. I believe in you. If I wanted something done in Jerusalem, I would say, 'Sahir, I have this to do.' And I know you would do it!"

Her credo for peace includes the solid conviction that no one is better than any other and that we must never get to the point of believing that strength wins and is the final solution to anything. For Sahir Dajani, the strong are obliged to help the weak; the educated, the uneducated. This notion has freed her to help whomever needs her gifts. It is not an exclusively Islamic idea, but she has discovered it and made it her own.

Notes

1. In the Middle East marriages have been arranged since before the days of Abraham. Technically, an arranged marriage means that two sets of parents do the looking for their children and arrange for a boy and a girl, who each have veto power, to marry. There are various customs attendant to such an arrangement, including the bride price, which the groom's family must pay. I knew of two young men whose bill for their bride price in 1988 was between ten thousand and twenty thousand dollars each. Sometimes, among the more modern, no bride price is exchanged.
2. Shuafat is the suburb where Mary Franji lives.
3. This Musa Alami is the same man who gave Hind Husseini five hundred dinars (see Chapter 3).
4. This was the first time I had heard her called Set Hind. I asked Sahir what *Set* meant. "Lady," she said. "Because you just can't say *Hind* plain. *Set,* that means a respected lady, a respected woman, because people cannot call her plainly; she is too great a lady for that."

10. MALAK SHARAF

I was so fearful. I remember the minute that they announced that it was war [the Gulf War]. I jumped off my bed. I went to my kids. I didn't wake them up but I was worried going from room to room, not knowing what to do. I wanted to do something. What if now a missile comes down? I remembered all these small things like putting carbonated water into water and shaking it to check for poison gas. My husband said, "Calm down. Nothing is going to happen." But he was scared, too.

Malak Sharaf

When the Gulf War began, most of us switched on CNN. Malak, a young mother living in Jerusalem, rushed from room to room in the middle of the night, feeling that there must be something she should be doing appropriate to the crisis. For so many of us, the minute-by-minute coverage was high drama, not unlike the plethora of apocalyptic films and television spectaculars that have become part of our "entertainment" diet. Perhaps some watched dispassionately. It was not dispassionate for those living it, however, and Malak and her family were living it.

Everyone, Israeli and Palestinian, had been told to prepare a sealed room in their homes as a refuge from the chemical warheads on Iraqi missiles. In that room they were to keep gas masks, telephones, food and water, a radio or TV, and books and games to occupy their time during air raids. During the first hours of news coverage, American networks vied to broadcast the latest developments. Americans phoned their friends in those sealed rooms to report that, if they had not already seen it on their own screens, another Scud rocket had been launched. How horrifying! This was not a TV drama. It was a matter of life and death. Sometimes it was hard to tell the difference, unless it happened to be your own life and the lives of your loved ones.

> I sealed my children's room, and we finally all went to it and jumped in their beds. We needed to be together with them, to comfort them and put those gas masks on. I used to make little jokes sometimes, saying, "Hey, we look like pigs." And once my daughter said, "Mommy, we look like ugly pigs. The pigs are pink and nice and they look better than we do."

Even though Malak's work was just across the street from her home on the west side of the Mount of Olives, she stayed at home with her family. School was not in session, so her two children, Nabil (then thirteen) and Nuha (then ten) were at home, and Malak wanted to be with them.

I was prepared mentally because I believed it was going to happen. My mother lived in Ramallah [a village only a few miles north of the city]. I called her the day before and said, "You'd better come and be with us so I won't worry." She replied that she was fine.

Then I said, "No, it's better for me, and if you love me, you'll come. I don't want to worry about you, and I don't want you to worry about the four of us." So she came, and that night the war started for us. I had had the feeling it was coming soon.

Before it happened, I asked my kids to open their masks and try them on so they could see how they worked and no accident would happen. They were laughing and saying, "Mom is so much prepared for war." Then I said, "Well, I feel it, and I believe it is going to happen." And it did. That night.

As the days turned into weeks, a new regimen emerged and the horrendous became commonplace. New habits were established. Families were thrown together in very close quarters for hours at a time. Relationships either blossomed or shriveled, and wrenching adjustments were necessary.

As time went on, it subsided a bit. The first week was fearful. Then it eased a little bit. We would listen to the news and try to laugh about some things, so the kids wouldn't be afraid.

After a few days, Malak walked the short distance to work and discovered that the whole Palestinian neighborhood had been invited to use the shelters in the large building that housed the Jerusalem Center for Near Eastern Studies. Not only that, but members of the Mormon church had come to the Center from Tel Aviv, where the most Scuds were dropping.

During this period, Israelis chided each other for being unpatriotic in moving inland temporarily to safer territory, fleeing the coast as it withstood a torrent of missiles. It was thought at first that Iraq would steer its missiles clear of such holy sites in Jerusalem as the walled Old City with its mosques, El Aqsa and Dome of the Rock. As the days went by, however, the Iraqis' accuracy came into question. Every place was at risk. To many it seemed more rational to flee for a time in order to live to fight another day. No one knew what strategy the next phase of the war might require.

Remarkably, the Israelis agreed to let the UN forces protect them. They were led by Americans, who had traditionally been strong allies for Israel, but this was the first Middle Eastern war since 1948 in which the Israelis had not masterminded their own defense and fought their own battles. It was with great restraint that Israel kept its army and air force out of the fray from one day to the next.

The first two weeks we didn't come to work, even though it was less than a five-minute walk. I could be home quickly. We were under curfew at first and then when they lifted the curfew, I came to look to see what was happening at the Center. I had my mask by my side. But it wasn't as bad as the first two weeks.[1]

How would one deal with the stress and fear such events engender? How can those who have never known war firsthand understand? What scars are left, and as a mother, how did Malak try to prevent wounds to her children's emotions?

I hid my feelings because I didn't want the children to be fearful, even though I knew they were. You can't help being afraid when you hear the siren, especially to be awakened in the middle of the night. Once it was like three or four times in one night. Oh, it was hard—running to a safe place and then coming back over and over again.

Malak shared her concerns with her husband, Sharif, and he talked with her about his fears. "I am also afraid," he told her, "but we shouldn't let the children see. We should be calm because of them and not let them feel our tension."

Malak felt she had been warned intuitively of the start of the war, that God had given her a chance to prepare and she had followed the promptings. It had not been the same for others.

At the time of the war I knew several people who were short of money. I asked one of them on the phone, "Did you prepare? did you store? did you get some food?" and she said, "Well, we don't have much money."

I felt so bad. I went to the store to buy things for me. Then I asked the shopkeeper to get me another box. He said, "Why do you need two boxes?"

I said, "Whatever I put in this box, I'm going to put in that box."

He asked why, and I said it was for a family I knew.

So I prepared two boxes. The same as I took for myself, I took for them. This was food to store in case the shops were closed. I took that other box and gave it to them. I felt so good.

Malak Sharaf was among the first Palestinian women I met when I came to Jerusalem to live. She is a Muslim but does not wear the traditional dress and veil. Perhaps this fact helped me be at ease with her more quickly. She is a beautiful woman, always dressed impeccably in colors that complement her dark hair and eyes. When I first met her, in 1988, she had just been hired to be a secretary at the Jerusalem Center where I was teaching.

I remember how kind she was, always able to think of ways to help. To say she was efficient would be true but inadequate. She seemed able to make things possible that at first glance appeared to be impossible. She could always find a solution. Her motto might well have been, "Why are we here, if it is not to make life easier for others?" She was—and is—a breath of fresh air.

I wasn't sure of the etiquette of the local culture, so it took a while for us to become acquainted, though I admired her from our first meeting. Soon it was apparent that because we were both outgoing women, in any culture we would be friends.

When I asked her to be part of my study of Jerusalem women, she asked who else I had interviewed. When she heard the name Hind Husseini, she blushed, saying she didn't belong in the same book. It took some convincing and detailed explanations for her to change her mind. She was willing to help, but she didn't feel as important as the other women I was interviewing, though few of them are known outside their own neighborhoods. As we discussed the matter, it became clear that everyone should be valued, no one being "more equal" than any other. All are alike unto God.

Malak's great-great-grandfather moved to Jerusalem about two hundred years ago from Bosnia (the former Yugoslavia). A Muslim and an architect, he moved to the city when restoration on the El Aqsa Mosque was underway. He intended to be there only a short time, just to help with the restoration. Instead, he married a Palestinian girl and settled down. Thus Jerusalem became his home.

Malak's grandmother lived across the street from the Albright Institute just off Saladin Street.

> When we were kids, we used to go and play at my grandmother's house. It had a fence exactly like the Albright. Then they took down the fence and put shops there, and they widened the road. But her house still stands, and my aunt Ayesheh Zayed is living there.

Malak was born in Jerusalem not far from her grandmother's house at St. Joseph's Hospital in Sheik Jarrah, an area northeast of the Old City. When she was about two or three years old—the third child in a family of seven—her family moved to Ramallah. She attended St. Joseph's, a good private school in Ramallah, where she was taught by Catholic nuns; her brothers attended the Friends' School there. She remembers her childhood as peaceful and normal.

> My father, Ahmad Karjawally, managed El Uma Bank in East Jerusalem. My mother, Kadija, was a pretty redhead and stayed at home to raise the children. Later she taught Islamic religion,

three courses, to the Muslims at that Catholic school. We were a
happy suburban family.

Malak's son, Nabil, remembers with joy how his grandmother
Kadija would gather the grandchildren around her. She would read
stories to them from the Koran about Abraham, Moses, Mohammed,
and Jesus. It was from his grandmother's reading that Nabil remembers learning for the first time about the prophets.

Malak wants her children to learn just as she learned at her mother's knee and in the world as well:

After I graduated from St. Joseph's School in Ramallah, I studied
administration at the UNRWA Center for Training Women that
was sponsored by the United Nations. There I studied accounting
and sharpened my secretarial skills. It was a three-year course,
and I tested out in English and shorthand for a higher certifica-
tion. In 1970 they sent me to London for nine months to get fur-
ther training in English and shorthand. I was nineteen. The three
diplomas they gave me in English, shorthand, and typing are
from the Royal Society of Arts.

After her training, at age twenty, she went to work for a tourist
agency, Shepherd's Tours and Travel, a venerable agency in the Holy
Land. Tourism is big business in Israel. A handsome young man
named Sharif would come by the agency, and she began to notice that
he liked her.

They started seeing each other, contrary to Palestinian tradition.
Perhaps, had her father lived (he had died recently of cancer, at the
age of fifty-one), things would have turned out differently. Perhaps
not. The modern world crowds out some ancient ways. Still, the need
for their families to be acquainted persisted in their courtship.

He met my brothers and sisters and mother. My mother knew
Sharif's mother. They lived on the same street that we did when I
was two years old.

Our families were very much alike in their degree of devotion to Islam. We all fasted for Ramadan. My mother prays five times a day. Neither of our families wore the veil or insisted on conservative dress. It seemed like a good match.

We dated almost a year. We'd go to a small cafe in West Jerusalem [the Israeli side] and sit at "our table" and just talk and talk. It was at the beginning of Jaffa Road. Every day after work, Sharif was waiting for me.

On October 1, 1976, we were married in Jerusalem. It was a small ceremony, and a Muslim judge from the Religious Court officiated. All the dowry arrangements were made, but my family never accepted money for their daughters. It was all symbolic—one golden English pound was my dowry. I remember my father saying, "My daughters are not for sale."

I wore a white dress and veil. We had the party at the Ambassador Hotel on the hill near the Palestinian Embroidery, which the Mennonites run. There was no dancing at the reception, just soft music, a small buffet with soft drinks, and a wedding cake. It was very simple and nice. The invitations were unique because we said, "Please bring children." Children were not usually invited to such affairs.

Children were welcomed into the new family as well. Malak continued working until one month before their first child, Nabil, was born on July 9, 1977. After her son's birth, she stayed at home. Three years later their daughter, Nuha, was born on July 3, 1980. Mothering became Malak's joy, and she cultivated the arts required of a homemaker. She enjoyed cooking and keeping a home for her husband and two children. They were the center of her life.

Nabil, her son, remembers how she used to knit their sweaters, not just to save the money but because it was a labor of love to clothe her children against the winter cold:

We loved waiting for our sweaters to be done. Every day we would ask, "When will my sweater be finished?" It was wonder-

*ful to anticipate, very different from going to a store and buying
something warm for winter. We could even pick out the designs,
and she would go to the store and pick out the colors. Each winter there was a new sweater. We had tons of sweaters. It brings
back such wonderful memories.*

In Jerusalem, women at home cook all morning to prepare the
noon meal. This is the traditional time for the main meal of the day.
How good the many different meals smell in almost any neighborhood if you chance to be there around noon! Malak is a great cook.
She cooks large portions, yet Nabil remembers very few leftovers. He
can also recall each day as a different experience of eating, and always
it was delicious. Sharif sometimes cooked breakfast and supper, but
Malak never let anyone else cook the main meal. That was her
domain.

When Nuha was eight and Nabil was eleven, Malak crossed the
street to apply for a job at the recently completed Jerusalem Center
for Near Eastern Studies. For three years the beautiful building had
been slowly rising in full view of the little village where she lived.
Naturally, the neighbors were curious about the large structure, sup-
posing it to be an Israeli government building. When they learned
that it was a private institution, they were surprised. It was being
built on land that had been part of Jordan before the Six Day War and
thus was thought of by the Palestinians as expropriated. But an
American university was preferable in some small way to the Israeli
government moving in next door to their Arab village. When Malak
learned about the university, it made sense to see if jobs might be
available. She began working at the Center in 1988.

Students and teachers had moved into the new Center on the
Mount of Olives on March 9, 1987. The ultra-orthodox Jews in Mea
Shearim had opposed the Center strenuously, so the move had been
quickly accomplished the moment the permission to occupy had
been granted by the municipality.[2] One day the workmen were everywhere, and the next day students and faculty moved in their belongings as well as the library books and equipment. The day after that,

classes began. It was into this milieu that Malak came a few weeks later to help set up the official procedures of the semester-abroad program sponsored by Brigham Young University in Provo, Utah.

For the most part her job was pleasant. She worked in a clean, beautifully designed space with breathtaking views of the Old City. She appreciated and grew to love her associates, who reciprocated those feelings. She regularly cut roses from the gardens to put in small vases around the office, and she always kept one on her desk.

Surprisingly, the short walk from her home was sometimes difficult.

It had to do with the necessity of walking past the Israeli soldiers who were often near the lower gate of the Center. Part of the road just outside the gate was often blocked by burning tires, a common protest of young Palestinians during the first Intifada, and Israeli soldiers were often stationed there. She was afraid of these young Israelis with their khaki uniforms, guns and bulletproof vests.

They teased her—harassed might be a better word—using crude language that embarrassed her. She was afraid to ask her husband or son to accompany her for fear of what the soldiers could do to them. Day after day, as she took the short walk to work, she hoped they wouldn't be there. Sometimes they weren't.

A reality of life in Jerusalem during the first Intifada was the torching of cars and the stoning of any moving vehicle on West Bank highways. Early one evening, Malak and her husband and their two teenage children were on their way to a concert. Along the steep road that leads from their home to the crest of the Mount of Olives, stones suddenly began to rain down on the Subaru taxi in which they were traveling. Several boys were hurling the stones, but they saw only one lad, who jumped in front of the car to throw his missile and then jumped back. Nabil said he thought the car would surely hit the boy, but it didn't. The driver tried to avoid the stones by swerving into the left lane, narrowly missing a car coming down the Mount. Half the windows in the car were smashed, but they kept going. They couldn't stop, because no one knew how many more stones would be thrown. And with the car windows mostly gone, further stones would be lethal.

Sharif, who was sitting in the right front seat, had most of the shattered glass on his shoulders and lap. Luckily, nothing hit his face or head, but a large stone bruised his arm. Nabil had glass in his lap, as well. They arrived at the concert hall, washed up, and went on with their evening plans. They were shaken, but in this city, such events have unfortunately become commonplace. One goes on with one's life.

Not long after this experience with her family, Malak and I had just picked up the bag of mail for the Center at the East Jerusalem Post Office. As we drove through the crowded, noonday traffic up Saladin Street, stones the size of baseballs began pelting our small Subaru.

It is not a pleasant memory, but we laugh about it these days when we recall our outcries as the first stones hit. She yelled out to our invisible assailants, "Open your eyes! Can't you see I'm a Palestinian!" while I cried out to her, "I'm not afraid! Are you?" Of course the adrenaline was pumping, and we fled as quickly as possible. The strangest thing I recall was that none of the Palestinians on the bustling sidewalks seemed to notice the thudding that sounded like small explosions inside our car. As we drove past the crowds of men, women, and children, we could not identify who was throwing the rocks. All drivers were accustomed to watch roadsides for young people with stones in their hands to avoid such a potential barrage, but in this crowded business district the stone throwers were invisible.

We drove to the bottom of the street where the traffic and people thinned out and pulled over to the side of the road across from a pottery shop. Quickly we got out of the car to examine the damage. We both realized, however, that it was not the damage we cared about, but being trapped inside the moving car. It was that feeling of claustrophobia that caused us to jump from the car at the first possible moment. No broken windows—a kind of miracle—and a few dents in the roof and hood were all we discovered. As we stood looking at each other, we began to laugh. We were still very scared, but when the adrenaline wore off, we drove back to the Center with the mail—and a tale to tell.

In such a setting Malak speaks of her hope for peace. She prays for peace. But more, she prays that her children will come home from school safely. This is a day-to-day concern. Whether Israeli and Palestinian leaders finally settle their differences and move forward in the peace process matters mightily, but from one day to the next, her concern is for the well-being of her family. She is not watching the peace process from afar. She is in the middle of it.

The last couple of days were really tense in our village [October 12, 1992]. It was tense everywhere. I was waiting for my kids to come from school. I was worried because of what's happening all over Jerusalem. They couldn't phone and reach me or Sharif. Then at 3:30 P.M. I tried to reach my husband. He was looking for the kids. He went to the school and brought them. The minute they arrived, we went to have lunch. I set the table, and we sat down and relaxed. Suddenly, my son said, "Something is happening over there." So I looked from the window, and I saw this car on fire, just near our house.

I was really scared. We all went to the window, and the IDF [Israeli soldiers] came. Then I saw all the IDF going from door to door, taking all the boys out and putting them against a wall. I looked at my husband, and he understood very quickly. He said, "Do you want that we leave the house?" I said, "Yes, let's do it." So we left lunch on the table.

We went straight to the car and drove to his sister's for a visit. We didn't eat. We just left for a couple of hours. When we came back they told us that they went to all of the houses, and took all of the boys and put them against the wall for two hours. They took some and left some. It's often someone who comes into the neighborhood who does these things, not one of the boys who lives here. They come in and out in a hurry and no one sees them. It's hard for the IDF. It's hard for the boys. It's hard for everybody. Can you imagine the worry I feel as a mother?

So that was really scary. That's our daily life. It was a horrible day.

In contrast, Malak spoke quietly of her faith in the future.

I have the faith that the situation will change. I love the idea of peace. I pray for peace. I believe in our two peoples living together and not fighting. They've done it before. They can do it again. If the people have enough willpower, it will work.

When I feel sometimes in danger, or I'm really concerned about one of my kids coming from school, I pray for God to help them and be with them.

We have these small prayers. I always say them, small prayers from here and there in the Quran. I learned those from my mother. She always does them. I teach them to my kids when they are in the time of sorrow or a time of danger. I teach them to say these and they feel comfortable and everything goes smoothly.

This is an example of one of them:

"Our Lord, take us not to task if we forget, or make mistakes.

"Our Lord, charge us not with a load such as Thou didst lay upon those before us.

"Our Lord, do not burden us beyond what we have the strength to bear.

"And pardon us, and forgive us, and have mercy on us; Thou art our protector."

Malak and her children take strength from the feeling that God will be their shield and protection.

When I asked her how the children on both sides of the conflict could possibly be taught to live beyond the fear and distrust that they've grown accustomed to, she was quick to reply:

We must teach our children at home. It we teach them well, they can learn to trust again. I teach my children that this is possible. It must begin at home and then move to the schools, but things like this start at home. It is the attitude of the parents that makes the difference.

She had sent her son to a special camp in which Israeli and Palestinian youth lived and worked together. The idea was that they could enjoy being together and live in peace on a small scale and that this could translate into real life when they returned home. Such retreats are run by organizations who see the possibility of peace emerging from the grass-roots, apolitical·mixing of young people, allowing them to learn from their own experience that all of us are basically alike, seeking peace and freedom and dignity.

As Malak thinks of the future, she can picture a time when the turmoil is finally finished:

> *It will feel so different when we feel that we are doing things our-selves, that nobody is ruling us or forcing us to do things. It will feel like we are "out of jail." Our lives have been so complicated during this long struggle. We want it to be better for our kids.*

Her dreams of the future include seeing her children well educat-ed. That dream is in process of coming true. Her son, Nabil, attends Brigham Young University on a scholarship and will graduate in com-puter science. Her daughter, Nuha, is already being recruited to come from Jerusalem to the University of Southern California or to any of several other schools. Nabil's hope that his sister would join him at BYU was interrupted when Nuha fell in love and got married. Her marriage was also a departure from tradition but one in which her mother delights.

Malak spoke of her hope in the future:

> *I'd like to be with Sharif when my kids leave. This has always been my dream. I pray that no harm comes to either of us. I love him, I love to stay with him always. It will be wonderful to see my kids in their own homes, happy and married.*
>
> *We believe in another life after this one, in heaven. I hope I'll be with him again there.*

She told me a tender story about when she was trying to decide whether to marry Sharif:

When I got acquainted with Sharif, and fell in love and we were dating, I talked with my mom. I had said yes to him, but I wanted my mom to say yes, too. She said, "OK, if you feel he is good. I felt he was good from his first coming to us and to our home." Then she said, "What do you need me to do?" And I said, "Pray and see me in your dream tonight." Because sometimes she said that she prayed and saw me. She woke up the next morning and she said, "Go ahead and get married to this good man." I said, "Did you see me?" She said, "Well, I saw you with him in heaven, holding hands. You were wearing a white, flying dress. He was holding your hand, and you were running on a green, green lawn together." It was so special. I still remember this and so does my mom.

Malak's hopes and dreams and simple faith visibly sustain her, and with them intact, she sustains those around her. Her caring, gentle ways reflect her faith in a future where others will learn gentle ways. Absorbing hurt and continuing to be kind and good breaks the chain of evil in the world. This has always been her habit.

It is not easy. In her job, personnel is constantly changing: students, faculty, and even administrators go back and forth from the States. The only sure thing in her office is change. Still, she learns to love each one, including hundreds of students she knows she will likely never meet again once they return to their homes. Yet, in her own sphere, she creates the miracle of peace over and over again each day.

Notes

1. Curfew, which forbids residents to go out of their homes or villages, has been a common practice in the West Bank imposed by the Israelis to counteract terrorism or, on occasion, merely to demonstrate their power.
2. The ultra-orthodox Jews were afraid that a university center sponsored by The Church of Jesus Christ of Latter-day Saints would be nothing more than a place from which proselytizing would take place. The university signed an undertaking not to proselytize and has kept that agreement scrupulously.

11. SHARON ROSEN

I went from Ireland to Russia. We call it in Hebrew Shelichut, or service in behalf of the Jewish community. I saw this as a mission to the Jews. That's what mission means to me. We traveled into Russia in 1984 taking things for the Jewish refuseniks, goods they could sell: kosher foods for prisoners, literature, like prayer books. We also went to ask what they needed. It was secret work. A bit dangerous, as we could have been expelled.

Sharon Rosen

Baka village, south of Jerusalem near the road to Bethlehem, is a wonderful mixture of Sephardi and Ashkenazi Jews, some of whom have
lived there for six or seven generations. The shops are owned by families who have been offering their services for fifty or sixty years, at
least. And they still think of themselves as offering service.
Shopkeepers shout greetings to passersby or invite them into their
shops for samples. Sharon Rosen relates:

> *I went into the laundry the other day, a new one that I haven't
> tried before, and the man said to me, "Haven't you ever been here
> before? I've been here for fifty years." The shopkeepers are like
> that, very friendly and warm. They chat with you, and they talk
> to you about their families. They even greet you on the corner.
> The local baker gives you a cake to taste or a bureka to try out.
> They do this regularly. It has a lovely feel about it.*

It was April 27, 1993, a Tuesday, and we were lunching at a quaint
open-air restaurant on a busy street not far from the neighborhood
where she lived. We had been casual friends for some years, and I had
always admired her. On this spring afternoon she agreed to guide me
through some of her personal history.

Her casual revelation of her clandestine visit to refuseniks in
Russia is part of this history.[1]

> *Ireland was a favorite country from which to send people
> because of its neutrality. I was approached by the Israeli
> Embassy to go to Leningrad, as it was called at that time. My
> husband, David, couldn't go because of his high profile position
> as chief rabbi of Ireland, so I chose to go with a female friend. I
> went for a week in 1984.*
>
> > *I don't know if "mission" is quite the right word. Quite a few
> > Jewish couples were being sent from different parts of the world
> > to visit refuseniks. The point was to give them emotional support,
> > to show they had not been forgotten. The practical reasons were
> > to take in goods for their religious needs and other goods that*

could be sold on the black market. The proceeds would be used
to support these people, who had lost their jobs and were often in
prison.

It was exciting but not too dangerous. The worst that could
have happened would have been immediate deportation. As it
was, we carried out our intentions and managed to leave some
very expensive equipment behind.

Her revelation took me completely by surprise. This beautiful
young woman with her gentle English accent, so elegant, proper, and
well bred, traveling to Russia before the breakup of the Communist
regime—and suggesting it was "not too dangerous." I saw her with
new eyes. She had been willing to take risks in the days when Jews
were captive in Russia because she viewed it as her personal contri-
bution to her people.

As we ate our vegetarian lunch together, she shared more details
of her life:

I was born in London, England, on July 15, 1953. I attended a
Jewish primary school in London until I was ten years old. There
were no decent Jewish high schools for girls in those days, so I
took the tests to qualify for an English grammar school. I passed.
I attended a Protestant grammar school until I was fifteen. My
father had decided to retire and come to Israel the next year, in
1970, so I had to hurry to finish my schooling because I wanted
to emigrate with my family. I did my "A" levels for matriculation
in college which normally would have taken two years, but I
completed the work in one. I finished school very early, at the age
of sixteen.

My family settled in Tel Aviv in July, while I lived in
Jerusalem so that I could study at the Hebrew University. I lived
here from September 1970 until August 1973.

That was not an easy time to come to Israel—but has there ever
been an easy time? The years after the Six Day War were character-

ized by growth and patriotic pride, a kind of celebration of the war of miracles for the Jews that had enlarged Israel's borders to include the "other half" of Jerusalem. Now Israelis could joyously speak of a united city. Before that time, they had only been able to gaze across a no-man's land toward the Western Wall, their holiest site. Now they could visit it.

This was when the world began to hear of the Jordanian West Bank. Israel had become an occupier, a stance that the fledgling nation has struggled with ever since. The country was still expanding in more than borders. It was a good time to make *aliya* (literally to "come up," which is the way one always speaks of immigrating to Israel), although committing to live in Israel as a Jew is dangerous, even if it is a "coming home." No one ever speaks of it in quite that way, however, at least no one who has chosen to live there.

Living in Israel was the key to Sharon's meeting her future husband, a rabbi:

> *David and I met as a result of my mother's determined efforts to get us together. She didn't know him personally but had heard about him and his illustrious family. She worked on common friends to drop tidbits about me in his and his mother's ears.*
>
> *I, of course, refused to meet a rabbi, but he phoned me one day whilst I was home visiting my parents in Tel Aviv. My mother immediately cottoned on to who was at the other end of the phone and confused me so much with her simultaneous persuasion to accept his offer to go out that I relented. She also offered us spare tickets to the Israeli Philharmonic that she had on the evening he wanted to take me out.*
>
> *David, of course, was very impressed with my musical offer, came to Tel Aviv on weekend leave from the army, picked me up from the house, and it was love at first sight—that is, my mother fell in love with him immediately and has remained his greatest fan ever since. It took David and me about two days more. We were engaged five weeks later and married four months later, whilst he was still serving in the army as an army chaplain and*

I was in the second and middle year of university. I was nineteen.
He was twenty-one.

The photos of this handsome young couple during their wedding festivities depict the celebration that was possible in the emerging nation of Israel just a few months before the Yom Kippur War in 1973. Sharon paints a captivating picture of her wedding day:

We were married at the Tel Aviv Hilton in May 1973. We had wanted to get married in Jerusalem, at the Hebrew University amphitheater on Mount Scopus overlooking Jordan, but my parents won the day and held the wedding in their town. As they were footing the bill, I guess they had first choice.

We were due to get married at sunset on the outdoor patio overlooking the sea, but a strong wind developed and started blowing the flowers all over the place so we had to move it inside. I swore that my wedding would be punctual, but it began half an hour late because of that wind.

But the flowers were beautiful. I had wanted red and white, but the florist refused, saying those colors were used for Israeli funerals. In the end I had burgundy and white blossoms, which I also wore in my hair as a fresh flower coronet.

With about 350 people attending, the wedding could not have been considered a small, intimate affair. Her memories of particulars blur a bit, as would any bride's, but the things she recalls are touching:

I remember loads of Israeli dancing (men and women separately) and not eating anything. Every time I returned from dancing, the food had been removed from my place. There were quite a few speeches and some harmonious singing—David together with his two brothers. His oldest brother married us, and the second brother read the marriage contract under the chupa [marriage canopy].

Another memory of the wedding was my father being taken home in a wheelchair at the end. Whilst dancing rather wildly,

The Rosen family

he fell and slipped a disc in his back. He must have been in agony but didn't let on until the end.

Part of Sharon's security, if not all of it, is in her family:

I've really learned that my roots are my family, and if I can take them with me, that makes a very, very big difference. And also, having gone abroad to live in Jewish communities, I've always felt that I was going to something familiar.

We lived in Johannesburg, South Africa, from September 1973 to the end of 1974. David was a chaplain to the Jewish students on the university campuses. Yakarah, our oldest daughter, was born there in May 1974.

We lived in Cape Town from 1975 until July 1979 while David was senior rabbi of the Sea Point Synagogue (ten thousand congregants). Gabriella was born there in November 1976.

We lived in Dublin, Ireland, from November 1979 to January 1985 where David was chief rabbi, after which we returned to Israel. Amirit was born there in February 1982.

Sharon, her husband, and their three daughters visited the Jerusalem Center for Near Eastern Studies to demonstrate a typical Shabbat evening meal for Rabbi Rosen's students. A handsome and cohesive family, they were obviously having fun together. Because they are orthodox and keep kosher, their food was specially prepared. They stayed the night in the Center guestroom because they lived far across Jerusalem. Their travel home would have been much farther than the permitted Sabbath journey.

What good fortune for us! We shared most of two days with them, witnessing their observant living and their joy in each other and in everyone else. We heard them sing in wonderfully strong harmonies the traditional songs that enliven their holy day. Their voices blended like a quintet that had practiced hundreds of times, which of course they had. As each song melted into the next, one could almost hear their ancestors singing the familiar tunes.

Rabbi Rosen and Sharon took turns embracing each of their daughters, intoning a mother's and a father's blessing in whispered Hebrew phrases. It was a beautiful Sabbath connection repeated weekly. The blessings of their ancient foremothers, Sarah, Rebekah, Leah, and Rachel were invoked for the Rosen daughters. As the parents tenderly enfolded their children in their arms and their prayers, the hearts of the watching students were deeply touched.

This weekly ritual demonstrates a distinguishing feature of the Rosen family, who see themselves as pioneers of modern Jewish orthodoxy. In Judaism, it is customary for a mother to make a silent prayer for her family as she lights the Sabbath candles each week. That action signals the beginning of the Holy Sabbath in her home. But joining her husband in blessing her children is a modernization of ancient practice. It may compare to the bat mitzvah for girls, which has come to be practiced in modern times as a counterpart to the ancient rite of bar mitzvah for boys.

Sharon explains the traditional view of women's responsibilities in speaking of the set prayers offered in Judaism:

Bronze statue of a father's blessing in the Rosen living room

I came late to recognizing prayer as a personal obligation because Judaism does not encourage women to pray. Women are not counted amongst the quorum (minyan) of men needed for communal prayer and are not required to pray thrice daily. As a general rule, women are exempt from positive laws, which are time bound. It's a practical thing. It is recognized that if you've children to look after, you might not find time to pray in the morning—if you're changing nappies, or feeding, or whatever you might be doing that takes your time and energy.

I grew up in the sort of Jewish society where women did not have the same standing as men within the public domain. It's only lately, over the last few years, as my own Jewish feminism has grown, that I have sought a more assertive religious role for myself and to set an example for my daughters.

The idea of equal parenting in religious matters is a joint effort on the part of both Sharon and David. Her affection and respect for her rabbi-husband are an ever-present value in her life: "I have good friends. I have close friends; but the only person I really confide in is David."

David taught a course on the history of Judaism at the Jerusalem Center for Near Eastern Studies. His counterpart, a Palestinian professor, taught a companion course on the history of his people in the land. As might be imagined, this combination of Palestinian and Israeli could have been explosive. David Rosen ensured that it was not. A charming man, he and his diplomatic gifts have been used at the Vatican for more than a decade. He has made many trips there, and when Pope John Paul II visited Jerusalem, David Rosen was deeply involved in the visit.

Sharon, who began by team-teaching a class at the Jerusalem Center, now teaches a class she herself designed. Her course is entitled "Jewish Family and Culture." In this setting, she has the opportunity to practice techniques she has been teaching elsewhere.

She is definitely not the stereotypical rabbi's wife or the orthodox Jewish woman one sees on the streets of Mea Shearim. She does not cover her hair, as do many orthodox women. Her hair is beautifully styled and she is always impeccably dressed in the latest style. One would have been tempted to say on first meeting that this beautiful woman likely couldn't boil water. In fact, however, she is a fabulous cook.

Once when she had invited my husband and me to join her family for the Shabbat evening meal, I mentioned that we had some guests visiting us at that time. To my delight, she responded, "Bring them along. You know me, Ann. Once I begin cooking for Shabbat, we can accommodate any number!" Her Shabbat table indeed stretches as far as it needs to for both friend and stranger.

Not only that, her wonderful meals are strictly vegetarian, in keeping with a decision the Rosens made twenty years ago. In some ways, this decision has simplified her life—there is no need for the separation of meat and milk in the kitchen required by orthodox Judaism. In other ways, it complicates her life—or, as she would likely say, it challenges her creativity.

Her talents go far beyond cooking delicious food. Like the virtuous woman cited in Proverbs, Sharon uses the full range of her abilities to bless the lives of those around her, not only her family but the wider world as well. For instance, she teaches businesspeople and educators about a new learning theory. She told me how that came about:

> I went back to do a master's degree in English literature. I had graduated in political science and English literature. I hadn't majored in psychology; I fell into this work. I was offered a position as an assistant to a businessman who wanted help with certain educational projects he was sponsoring. He asked me to administer one particular project, which was this one. He fell in love with the project when he found out about it in the States and wanted to bring it to Israel in order to better Israeli society and education.

She took a brief training course in the United States to prepare her to teach others in Israel.

> I am administrating this program in Israel, which was created by a clinical psychologist by the name of Sandra Seagal, an American from Los Angeles.[2] Ms. Seagal is working in many different countries with this concept, which identifies people according to personality dynamics that cross sex, age, and culture.
>
> What is interesting about it is that by recognizing a person's dynamic, one is able to identify much more clearly the way the person thinks, feels, communicates, learns, and teaches. As a result, one can learn to communicate better with people, to understand why a person communicates the way he does and not be biased against him because he doesn't communicate in the same way you do. Sometimes one may think a person is unfeel-

ing, for example, when his mode of communication simply differs from one's own.

Sharon has seen in the world around her needs that were going unfulfilled. And she knows she has the ability to help:

This program has great relevance in schools, where our main work is being done at the moment, because we are teaching teachers to recognize that children learn in different ways.

Because eighty percent of the western world are of a particular type, most of the teachers teach in the way that that type learns. There are a minority of people who simply cannot learn that way. That doesn't mean that they are less intelligent, though. What this program does is make the teacher more sensitive to the needs of the children who are different from themselves [the teachers], and it provides teachers with tools to maximize the potential of those children.

It is also a way of maximizing team potential in businesses. We take teams of people who are working together and teach them how to integrate their communication skills.

Although she shoulders more and more responsibility for administering this program, her family remains her focus. Often, the demands of her profession and her responsibilities at home make Sharon feel as if she is being pulled in a tug-of-war. Within a few years, however, her priorities will change as each daughter leaves home. The older two have already served their compulsory time in the Israeli army, and Yakara, the eldest, was recently married. Sharon observes:

My role is changing. I recognize how much my work has really taken on in my life. I have a struggle as to how much I should let it take on and how much I shouldn't. Just last night I came home close to eleven and I had so much to do. I phoned you first and then I phoned somebody else and she said to me, "What does

*Amirit do by herself all day?" It struck me. Every night I'm out
till nine o'clock now and it is something I would never have
allowed myself to do before.*

*What has happened is that I have gotten to the age I do not
need to stay home for my children and now it's a personal choice
of how much I devote to my work and how much I devote to
them. It's a hard decision.*

Sharon often speaks of having been abundantly blessed.

*I'm very fortunate in the way that I live. My children are good
children. They've never caused me any problems. I'm very fortunate in that regard. You have to look at the economic situation,
too. We're not rich, but we have everything that we need. We're
comfortable. There are plenty of people in the world, and in
Jerusalem in particular, who are really suffering. I think of some
Palestinian women here, but I'm ashamed to say that I really
don't know many Palestinian women well.*

She speaks with deep feeling of concerns she had experienced
earlier in her life:

*I worked as a marriage counselor for five years in Ireland. That
gave me some sort of counseling base. It was an interesting time
for me. Ireland was a country where there was no divorce at all,
and I trained with the Catholic Marriage Advisory Council. I
worked within the Catholic society, although I was also there to
serve the Jewish community. Working with the Catholics in their
offices was a tremendous eye-opener.*

*I specialized in marriage counseling of couples who were
already married. But I did do some training in pre-marriage
counseling. I worked with adolescents and youth. I also worked
with natural family planning methods. It really took in the whole
gamut of family counseling. In the midst of it I worked in a
Jewish school.*

Sharon's quiet confidence surely was an asset as she served others in Ireland, where the Rosens lived while David served as chief rabbi. Life there was somewhat similar to life in Israel. Christianity had claimed adherents very early in Ireland; today, the feud there between Catholics and Protestants continues unabated. This chapter in her life prepared her for the role she now plays as the wife of a rabbi in Jerusalem.

Sharon's experiences represent those of most modern Israeli women. She has known uneasy peace in Israel. She has lived with the threat of war and with its reality. The Gulf War brought challenges, not the least of which was the interruption of schooling for the children, who had to remain at home, always ready to hurry into their "sealed rooms." During that time, she worked with other parents to establish temporary home schooling:

> A group of parents arranged meetings for children, usually from the same class, in their homes. We didn't start this immediately because we were all very nervous about even going out and having our children away from us. But after a couple of weeks we realized that things were not too bad, particularly in Jerusalem. Children met in different parents' homes, and the mother usually taught them something.
>
> I taught them how to bake fairy cakes. It wasn't exactly academic, but it lent a kind of pattern to their lives. This arrangement was for Amirit, our youngest daughter. We did it for about a month.

Sharon's descriptions of the Gulf War are both enlightening and frightening:

> When I look back on it, the whole time of the Gulf War seemed like we were living in a dream, that we were in suspended animation, waiting, not knowing what was going to happen day by day. Nobody was working, no schools, no university. Our normal lives just stopped.

I must say that the children were well prepared by their schools, and they exuded an enormous amount of confidence. I didn't have to worry about them the whole time. I remember thinking, "I'm so lucky, I don't have any babies who I have to worry about and stick them in these special cots and keep them there."³ I didn't have any old members of the family who were disabled to deal with. I really was in a good position.

The ironic thing was that people watching on CNN knew before the Scud missiles actually hit Israel, and they were phoning to tell us the Scuds were coming over.

How incredible that such memories recede into the background in the rush of daily living when life returns to normal. Sharon easily speaks of her dreams for the future. She personifies the hope of many women:

Living in Jerusalem, I think my dreams are very much part of the country's as a whole. I dream of when we can live in this place without fear of a terrorist attack. I dream of being able to live side by side with our neighbors in happiness, sharing, like France and Belgium, living next to each other. I would really love that dream to become reality.

Also, I have a dream for a much more tolerant society, particularly in Israel where people are allowed to live the way that they want to live, where people show by example and don't try to coerce others to be what they want them to be.

I have personal aspirations—that my children grow up to be the sort of children I would want them to be. So far, they have fulfilled all my expectations, and I just hope that that will continue. I would like it if our children continued to be religious Jews with the values that we have. Although it wouldn't be terrible if they didn't, providing they remained good people.

I would like to live a life of fulfillment. Service is part but not all of it. It's a feeling that life is satisfying, that when you come to the end of it, you can look back and see that it was worthwhile.

She is busily engaged in doing many good things. The satisfaction she finds in her work is exceeded only by the joy she experiences with her husband and children:

It is in my relationship with David that I find peace. I generally tend to be a calm person, although both my dentist and doctor tell me I keep it all in because my teeth look as if I've ground them to nothing, and my back regularly tightens. Obviously I keep some of it in. But if you live a life of such comfort and ease with somebody, it creates internal peace. If you're comfortable and you're happy with somebody, then many things don't worry you that would worry and irritate other people. And you have someone to share it with and therefore big problems tend not to be so big.

When I asked how decisions were made in their family, she laughed.

I'm sure if you ask David that question, he would give you a totally different answer from me. Without a doubt he would say, "Sharon makes the important decisions in the family." But if you look at our history in an objective manner, you will see that all our big moves have resulted from David's work and his needs, really, but the decisions have been joint decisions. I think it's true that if I had been against going to Ireland, if I had been against going to South Africa, we wouldn't have gone.

But what about returning home to Israel and the situation she is in today?

I feel free within Israel and can do what I want to do, but since the Intifada [of 1987–1993], my movements are much more restricted. I used to go into the Old City without thinking twice. I wouldn't do that now. We have friends in Effrat [a Jewish settlement near Bethlehem]. I think many, many times before I take

*my car to go there. I allow my children to go there, and they go
on the public transport; I don't take the car there. There are many
places where I feel restricted.*

What does she think about the capacity of the peoples in the
region to change the status quo? Is there the will to do it?

Her answer illustrates her remarkable optimism:

*I think that we can create a big change. I have developed quite a
bit of confidence living with David. Maybe living with David, in
the way I live, has helped me come to this feeling. I think it's a
good way to live, and I think that it's important to set a good
example to others. I think that that can contribute to change, and
I've heard that it has. I wouldn't say that about myself, although
I see that David has touched and changed people's lives tremen-
dously. But sometimes people have said to me, "Coming to your
home and being part of that kind of life has helped us," and I
guess that it is a joint thing.*

Yes, it is a joint thing. The two Rosens have made lasting impressions on young college students whom they have taught both for-
mally and informally. Such teachers go with us wherever we go in life.
Among many other things, picturing a handsome, orthodox Jewish
rabbi and his lovely wife embracing their daughters by turn to bless
them is a scene all who have witnessed will remember and cherish.

Notes

1. Refuseniks were Russian Jews who wanted to live in Israel and had been refused
   permission to leave Russia. They refused to give up on their Zionist dream and
   were persecuted as a result.
2. "Sandra Seagal is founder and president of Human Dynamics International and
   executive director of Human Dynamics Foundation. Both organizations are

devoted to the development, empowerment and sustainment of individual and collective human potential." *Systems Thinker* 5, no. 4, reprint no. 05401.

3. During the Gulf War, there were special arrangements made for small babies in sealed rooms, and several babies were injured by the paraphernalia.

12. KARIN GOLLER CALVO

I was born in the very north of Italy into a big family, and when I was eleven or twelve, I started getting interested in things like the municipality, like rights and wrongs and how the world works. In other words, my mind went beyond the mountains.

I could not continue studies because financially it just wasn't possible, but I did not want to give up. It was just a matter of knowing that if I wanted to know more about the world, life, politics, I had to get it by myself. My father said he would not give me a penny, and my mother said, "Whatever you will do, wherever you will go, I know you will make it." So I left.

Karin Goller Calvo

My first encounter with Karin was an accidental one at the swimming pool at the Hyatt Hotel in Jerusalem. I had a summer membership and went each day to swim laps. I learned later that Karin lived a few doors up the street and swam in the late afternoons with her family. Only slightly aware of the mother, father, and toddler who settled in chairs next to mine one afternoon, I spent my drying-off and sunning time watching the adorable little girl, who looked to be little more than a year old. Her mother was a serious swimmer.

As Karin climbed out of the pool and dried herself off, her hungry little daughter toddled over and, whimpering a bit, asked to be fed. Without skipping a beat, Karin tossed a towel over her shoulder, gathered in her little girl, snuggled her close, and began to nurse her, peeking under the towel and cooing and laughing.

I liked her before she ever spoke to me. When she looked up and smiled at me, I mentioned something about how wonderful it is to nurse a baby. She nodded and said something like, "But you must think I'm a bit old for this." The thought *had* crossed my mind. She said she didn't want to wean her daughter yet; it was such a comfort to both of them. An extended discussion of what we found to be remarkably similar family values followed. We agreed to meet to swim and talk again.

Karin told me that she lectured in the Law School at Hebrew University and had a private law practice as well. Her husband was also a lawyer and traveled a good deal in his work. They had a son presently doing his army service, so there was quite a spread between their nineteen-year-old son and their only daughter, with three more sons in between.

I learned later, when we tried to have a formal interview—punctuated by stimulating conversation and the occasional request from one son or another needing help with homework—that she had written a study, with her husband, on the vital nuclear agreements that changed the complexion of the post–Cold War world: *The SALT Agreements: Content, Application, Verification.* She taught a course at Hebrew University Law School called "The Middle East Peace Process."

How does one prepare to teach such a class? Each day the situation changes, often dramatically. Karin explained that she devoured the daily news even more voraciously than the average Israeli, for whom the news is very serious business. It would not be amiss to say that Israelis are addicted to news. And for good reason.

During the Gulf War, for example, CNN was broadcasting the war play by play, like a football game, even giving exact locations of Scud missile hits before someone in the United States state department warned that they were aiding Saddam Hussein's efforts to pinpoint his targets. That kind of international coverage happens only occasionally, when something that the media in the rest of the world considers vitally important is happening. But in Israel, each day's happenings are vitally important because residents are living right on top of the powder keg. The sense that it could blow up surges and recedes but is never absent.

Israelis rush to their sealed rooms on the authority of a voice on the radio to escape possible chemical warheads zooming overhead or exploding nearby. They listen intently for updates on the state of their borders. In the north is Lebanon, where their sons fought and died until Prime Minister Barak fulfilled a campaign promise and pulled out the Israeli forces. In the south is Egypt, with whom Israel has an uneasy peace. In the east is Jordan, which is a partner for peace. In the east, too, is Syria, which remains intent on recovering the Golan Heights and is far from the peace table. Each of these borders has been the scene of bloody conflict in the recent past. When one hears an Israeli ask about the news, it is never idle conversation.

But when Karin teaches, she has more than each day's news on her mind. This lawyer, teacher, mother of five, author of the definitive work *The SALT Agreements* and defender of the underdog brings a lifetime's worth of education and scholarship to questions of peace, to the distinct benefit of her students and friends.

Karin began her real-life education by walking away, at age fifteen, from the security and simple expectations of her hometown to use only her own resources in seeking the life she now enjoys.

*I was born on October 4, 1947 in Kastellorotto, Italy, which is in
the very north of Italy, the German-speaking part of Italy. I lived
there up to age fifteen and a half. My family is a big family, a
good family and a nice family. We were twelve children.*

Karin speaks of her early life in Italy:

*I had seven brothers and four sisters. It was a good childhood. It
was a healthy one, a happy one, an active one. Full of responsibility and hardship, but a very happy one in spite of it.*

*From an education point of view, there was education for
boys and for men. Education meant that every man had to learn
long enough to be able to fill a good post or to have a successful
business.*

*Girls were supposed to be good and to comply and someday
get married. That was very difficult for me to take. I did not want
to give up learning. It wasn't even a matter of doing what my
parents didn't want me to do, especially my father. It was just a
matter of knowing that if I wanted to know more about anything—the world, life, politics—I had to get it by myself.*

And at only fifteen and a half, she left home to do just that,
equipped with the tremendous courage it took to follow her dream
out of her village and into the world. She had completed all the
schooling the village could provide, the primary and secondary
grades, and left to see what the world had to offer.

*I went to France and I worked in a store in the morning and stud-
ied French in the afternoon and then I studied throughout the day
and sold newspapers in the evening. I sometimes took care of elderly people during the night and studied during the day. When I
finished I got my secondary degree in French. I did the same in
England, working here and there. Any decent, honest work was
good for me. But I did sometimes have a month where I just ate
a little bread and an apple daily, and it was O.K. It didn't really*

upset me terribly. I kept contact with my family, I wrote to them. I didn't have enough money to call but I saw them, more or less, once a year.

The girl who longed to learn, to see through a window to the world, had chosen French and English to help her see what was outside. These were wise choices for the young German-speaking girl.

That was my first education. In fact, I have two. My first education was languages. I was a translator-interpreter, and I got my degree in that in England. After that I went to work three years in Rome, and I worked for the FAO [Food and Agriculture Organization], which is one of the UN specialized agencies. Then I went to New York because the UN asked me to work for them there.

She was in her early twenties and a guide at the United Nations when she met Michel Calvo:

I was in uniform and he had a day to lose in New York on his way to Harvard for postgraduate work. However, it was absolutely forbidden to make dates or whatever when you were in uniform, which of course I did not. But Michel was persistent checking on all the doors—there are about fifteen in the UN building—until he found me . . . and we got married a year after.

Michel was still at Harvard at the time, and traveled back and forth between Massachusetts and New York for several months. Eventually he transferred to New York University so that they could be closer.

We were both twenty-six when we returned to France. Because Michel was already a lawyer, he had to return to Paris to continue his profession. For me it did not really make so much change. I was used to change every so often.

Living on her own had been an education in itself, her third education. In that school she learned to cope with hardship and she recognized how important it was to her to have a family. All of this knowledge she stored for a time when she would rear her own children—in an atmosphere both akin to and different from her home as a child.

Karin's early experiences taught her that she had a huge personal capacity to work for what she wanted.

But how would having children mix with her studies at the Paris Pantheon Law School, part of the famous Sorbonne?

> *One day in France, I was doing my physical exercises and Michel and I were talking—I was already expecting David, my first son. We were joking, and Michel said "Well, you always said you'd love to study law, so why don't you do it?" I said, "Why not?" And I completed my doctorate ten years later.*
>
> *I went straight through and along the way had four children. I had a child three months before I enrolled in law. I had a child in the third year, I had a child in the first year of my doctorate, and I had a child in the fourth year of my doctorate, as well.*

Comparing Karin's experience with that of the usual law student who is immersed in legal theory and practice like a horse with blinders, I could see that Karin had a different perspective on herself, her family, and her studies.

> *It didn't affect my studies nor my being with the children. In fact, I loved it, all of it! Had I not been involved with the having and rearing of my children, I think I might have gone overboard in legal theories. I'm that kind of person. It would have been self-satisfying, but of course, I realized that after a certain point I was much into theory and did not have enough of my feet on the ground.*

There is nothing like a 2 A.M. feeding to keep your feet on the ground. There is nothing like a child needing your help with a

Karin and Naomi

scratched knee or two tiny siblings fighting with each other and calling for a lawyer-mother's arbitration to give you a realistic approach
to the life of the world that is swirling outside your door. You can talk
theories all you want, but a child doesn't have time for a five-year
cooling-off period such as some international agreements require.
The child's needs are "now" needs, and the role of his mother,
whether she is working at home or away from home, has an imme-
diacy that won't wait.

For ten years Karin juggled the deadlines of law school and graduate school with the needs of her growing family. She knew about filling her days to the very top with what she considered two joyful pursuits. Likely there were those along the way who told her that this
couldn't work. Her success in both careers proved them mistaken. In
1981 she completed her studies and began practicing law. "Oh yes,"
she told me, "it all came along very naturally. In fact, I loved all of it—
both of my careers." Her perspective was surely enriched by combining the two segments of her life so readily. Her fine mind could have

focused exclusively and successfully on the labyrinth of the law, yet her children and family life were a balance to her legal studies. Children allow us to fly far afield but then come back to land with our feet planted firmly on the ground, by asking a simple question that lets all the air out of our grand suppositions in a moment. Children can teach us much if we are willing to listen. Karin listened.

Ten years after she began her legal studies, Karin joined her husband in practicing law. Michel had been practicing law all along and suggested to Karin that she come to the office twice a week. She agreed, and soon became a partner in the firm.

In 1986 she adapted and translated her thesis to make it a book:

I had done a bachelor, master's, and what you call, I think, a Ph.D. In France you have to go through all this. That is why it took five years after the master's.

In 1986 *The SALT Agreements* was translated and published in English. Then Karin adapted it into a French version that came out in 1987. Karin's book had caught a historic moment when many things were changing radically:

To find the documents we ran from Moscow to Washington to get papers. They agreed, because of the difficulties involved and the size, that two people would work on it. So my husband and I worked on it. I did the publishing and much of the research. He put on his name, too, because he contributed to the basic writing.

He had commentaries, and he certainly participated very positively. As an experienced lawyer he would say, "This is not clear, put it differently."

Karin jokes that their marriage actually survived this period of collaborating and writing together. Not long afterwards, they and their family moved to Jerusalem.

Had a particular event prompted them to make *aliyah*?

The particular event was that from 1982 to 1987, every morning when my husband left he said he would like to go and live in Israel and he thinks that it is the best place for the children. And he's right, about that he is absolutely right. I can say that after seven years living here.

As if on cue, one of her young sons, just home from school, calls up the stairs to the study where we are working. She comments, "He really wants to make sure that I am here."

Security, constancy, stability; there are many notions which are put in danger by not living up to one's words. This applies to your family more than anyone else. Why do we think it's our families that we can play around with?

Why, indeed? Karin has been in touch with her family of origin often over the years. She returned home in 1996 for her father's funeral. In recent times she sent an ailing son "home to be healed by the mountains, the lakes and the fields of strawberries"—and he was. Family ties sustain her.

In our interview, Karin expressed a genuine gratitude for her present blessings:

What I have is really great. I appreciate each and every one of my children and my husband. I am not a person to be too much alone. I really like people.

The conversation took an interesting turn as we spoke of family security and, in the same breath, of moving to Israel to live. Among all the countries in the world, Israel is not vying for first place in the race for security. Tourism fluctuates madly each time a bomb goes off, or grinds to a full stop during warlike conditions, and yet this family chose to make this tiny country, which has been harassed by terrorists and wars, their home.

After having lived in quite a few countries, I realize that there is a clear line between right and wrong, between "should do" and "should not do" here. And then, of course, family values. I didn't come here for that. I found out afterwards that parents really have a role here.

Parents mean something. Parents are not those people that one should run away from as soon as possible; parents are something good, even when one is eighteen. There are values—I mean the fact of being Jewish makes more sense in Israel. Beyond its being good for the children, I think it's good for me, too, because of this feeling that this is where it's happening.

It's not somewhere else, it's here it's happening, and I do not long for another place. I do not have a feeling that I would like to be somewhere else, a feeling I have known for twenty or more years before coming here.

In Israel Karin had a definite sense of belonging. The young woman who left home at fifteen and a half had come home at last. Somehow the fact that home was a war-torn country under siege or bloodied by suicide bombs was insufficient to tip the scales away from Israel.

After twenty-five people died in the Bus 18 tragedy in February of 1996, however, Karin was uneasy. She had been waiting for a bus that was scheduled to leave at 7:00 A.M. for Tel Aviv. At 6:40 A.M., Bus 18 arrived at the central bus station—and the bomb exploded. Two buses blew up, and Karin saw it all. She described the dead and dying, the stench of burned flesh filling the air, the pieces of human bodies strewn about on the ground.

There was such an anguish in Israel after the buses were bombed and all those people were killed. Think of the parents of the children who died; their lives were shattered. We are all broken-hearted. We give and give in Israel because we want peace. Some things become so irrelevant. We are thinking of our children and their children.

Perhaps living in a nation whose security is constantly at risk contributes to this higher resolve to be involved in the future of one's children and grandchildren. There is no complacency here. Measures must be taken now to ensure that future. The yearning to provide a secure future for their children is common to both Israeli and Palestinian parents.

The conversation turned to Naomi, Karin's youngest child and only daughter.

She is really very much part and parcel of all this. Naomi was born in 1991, just a month after I finished my bar exams to become a lawyer in Israel. I remember being eight months pregnant when I passed the ninth exam. Naomi was born in Paris. I went back to give birth because I knew the doctor there and it was again a caesarian section, so we decided to do it with the same establishment.

Of her five children, three had been born by caesarian section. They had been big babies, and Karin is a small woman.

Naomi was born when Daniel was six years of age. I always wanted a girl. No, not always; that's not true. I first of all wanted a lot of boys.

And I sure got that, but to be honest all the way, when I found that the fourth would be a boy, I had a kind of feeling that this is probably the last one because of the caesarian section. It would have been nice to have a girl. So I had never had a girl. It took me just the time to walk down the steps and have to do something else and think something else to get over it, but my husband kept talking about it.

And then one day we decided, why not? So we planned to have her. She was nothing like an accident. How rich you are when you have a large family!

Each stage of Karin's professional life had been achieved simultaneously with bearing her children. Bearing a child can play havoc with hormones and emotions. Life may seem topsy-turvy for a while as a mother adjusts to supplying the needs of her newborn. Squeezing a baby's needs into the crowded basket of older children's demands on time and energy can be daunting. And often, too, a husband seems to need nurture at precisely the same moment. Karin seemed oblivious to the strain of these demands.

My children and profession were really linked. Every time there was a step forward professionally there were children at the same time. But this just proves that it is possible and that one does not exclude the other. Excellence in parenting does not mean the exclusion of the professional life. I cannot say that I am excellent in professional life but . . .

She certainly is. How is this juggling of roles possible?

If I would give you this week's schedule, you would know it all. I'm a lawyer in Israel and I'm a lawyer in France, but this week I am working on cases here.

The one this morning at the High Court is a pretrial, and the procedure starts with a judge. My case is before the president of the High Court. He will decide if we have to have a hearing. If the case is convincing enough, he might decide without a hearing.

There are a lot of cases coming up tomorrow for child protection. I was just writing a contract between France and Israel for cooperation. Then I will be teaching Wednesday and Thursday. At the university I teach law and international relations, third- and fourth-year courses for students . . .

I ask Karin whether she ever aspired to be a judge, but she has no plans to be on the High Court some day:

I never have time to make plans. I just make it through the day and make sure not to leave too much for tomorrow. That is all I can do.

Sometimes things happen and I notice suddenly and realize that it happened because of something I have set in motion. But I hadn't consciously done it to make it happen. Do you know what I mean? I do not really have long-term planning. I do not. I'm not a very good strategist, even, in the sense that my husband is. He plans. You could say I am flexible; I am taken down to earth every day very much.

That's part of mothering. Karin's dual role affects her life in all its aspects, and she achieves a golden balance of which she herself may not even be aware.

This does not prevent me from having very high goals and standards in my teaching. I am often being told that I do too much in order to teach more.

It's not just a matter of obligation. If I teach, why, let's teach something not just interesting but something right, a step ahead of what is written. If I just repeat what is written, what do I teach? They can read; they are not illiterate.

Such a valuable gift she gives to those she teaches—her students, her clients, and especially her children and their children. She will always be rushing "a step ahead of what is written" to teach not just something interesting but "something right." Those principles sustain her, whether she is preparing meals for her family, lectures for her students, or briefs for her hearings at the High Court. In her hurrying she takes little time for herself. She is a very attractive woman and dresses beautifully but does not seem to be overly concerned with her appearance.

Her credo is to fill each day to the top and then make it through the day, trying not to leave too much for tomorrow. It works. Her list

Karin and Ann

of tasks is long and never finished, but she knows when to stop. On many days she marks the stopping place with a swim.

How grateful I am that our paths crossed at that precise place! Now that I know the complexity of her life, it is astounding that she was content on that first afternoon to simply nurse her baby and chat with a stranger beside the pool.

Getting to know her has been immensely rewarding. She has a marvelous way of putting words to ideas. Women's lives are always begging for solutions, and Karin's solutions are impressive.

Here is a woman, a legal authority on nuclear disarmament, proud and frightened to have sons serving in the Israeli Defense Force, an army that is routinely on high alert. Her faith in the future of her tiny nation is rock solid. Her faith in the future of her family energizes her and fills her days. Her faith in herself began as she walked away from the safety of her Italian home and her family of fourteen with only the confidence of her mother to take with her. She has come with that faith intact to what appears to be one of the least secure places on earth. There she invents her own peace within the four walls she calls home.

13. DIODORA STAPENHORST

God gives us gifts and different talents, and we have to use them. Whether our help is needed by somebody, this is judged by God. We don't know. We have to do what we can all the time, at every moment. Whenever something comes up we have to give everything.

Sister Diodora Stapenhorst

One often sees nuns walking purposefully through the streets of the Old City of Jerusalem, immersed in their life's vocation of doing good. They are easily recognized by their long black habits or modest, simple dresses. Diodora, a Greek Orthodox nun, was twenty-eight years old when we met at a small luncheon during a symposium held in Brigham Young University's Jerusalem Center. She had come with a handful of Greek Orthodox nuns and priests to listen to one of the presenters, Elder Dionysios, deliver a paper on the Greek Orthodox beliefs about the nature of man.

It was a delight to sit with this group at lunch, discussing with them the search for human nature and comparing ideologies. Diodora had such presence as she sat across the table. I was captivated by her Madonna-like beauty and asked if I might take her photograph. She inquired of Elder Dionysios with her eyes if it would be appropriate, and he nodded. I took her picture and asked if she would allow me to interview her to complete my composite picture of women of peace in Jerusalem. Another unspoken question to Elder Dionysios and his nod of assent told me we would meet again. She graciously offered to come for me the following week.

Sweeping down the bright marble hallway of the Jerusalem Center in her long black robes, she made her own breeze as she approached. I greeted her with three Easter lilies, which contrasted stunningly with her black habit. Sister Diodora, those lilies in her hands, is a picture I shall never forget. Her youthful features were beautiful without a touch of makeup. Her fair face was framed by the nun's veil that hid her hair. When we had met the week before, I had not noticed that she was so young. Is the clothing of the cloistered celibate meant to eradicate age?

We drove across the top of the Mount of Olives to the Greek Orthodox Monastery called Little Galilee, just two minutes from the BYU Center. The old red car putted along, and I wondered if we might not have done better to walk. It was such a short distance, and she was certainly able. Later we would walk that same road across the mount many times, talking together nonstop. She always seemed completely at peace.

Diodora with lilies on the Jerusalem Center balcony

Only two Greek Orthodox women lived in the pleasant compound of the monastery, Sister Diodora and a novice, Eleni. Somehow I had expected many nuns to be housed in this lovely, peaceful spot. I was captivated. Probably part of my fascination was having at last entered the gate I had so often passed, curious about what was inside. Now I had been welcomed there. An Arab family who acted as caretakers also lived within the high wall, quite near the gate. We saw them as we drove up the long drive.

Sister Diodora showed me around a bit, and then we sat down at a table in the sunlight to drink cool lemonade and eat fresh, salty white cheese with crackers. As I look back on that idyllic day, I cannot really set a boundary between our pleasant conversation and the formal interview. It was as if I had always known her.

She was born August 21, 1964 in the center of Germany, in Göttingen, about four hours from Frankfurt and three hours from Hamburg. She spoke fondly of Göttingen, a very old university town, full of students, with a famous law department. The climate there was cold and rainy:

I lived in Göttingen for the first ten years of my life as part of a family with six children and my father, who's a heart surgeon. He was called to a university very close to the French border to become a professor and the director of a new heart surgery department. The family moved with him, and I lived six more years of my life in Hamburg, close to Saarbrucken.

When I was sixteen, I left my family, because I had applied for an international college in England to do my two last years of high school. I learned English and had my first experience far away from home with international students. It was a boarding school and it was a very, very important experience for me.

How had she come from Germany and England to live on the Mount of Olives in Jerusalem? And how had this daughter of Lutheran parents chosen the life of a Greek Orthodox nun?

Both my parents gave us deep belief through the way they were living and through their values. They were Lutherans. We did not go very often to church when I was small. But I remember my father always reading theological books. He had a few Protestants that played a big role for him in his life—like Bonhoeffer. So I got this hunger to search very much from them. But what they gave was not enough for me. They created a search in me to look for more and to believe that there is something very high, deep, and everlasting.

I soon learned that the search for something "very high, deep, and everlasting" is characteristic of Sister Diodora. One could feel the hunger in her spirit. Her exploration had only just begun; she had no sense of having found all that she sought, but life itself was a quest to which she was deeply committed.

When I finished the high school in England, I went back to Germany and I started to study the history of arts in the university in Regensburg, a very old, Roman city, in southeast

*Germany. I studied there for two years and was very successful.
I liked it very much, but soon I felt inside that it was not what I
was really looking for and I felt that I wanted to do more with
my hands—and do the real art. I decided to apply, with a portfolio of my works, to the academy of Fine Arts in Berlin.*

*I moved to Berlin and prepared myself for entrance exams,
which were quite tough, but I got through and studied there for
three and a half years. It's a very old institute, very big. Berlin
was the center of the art scene. I was into everything completely,
and I lived very intensively. All my life was art, and I was working from the morning to late in the evening in my studio at the
school. I took it very, very seriously. I didn't know anything else,
just art. This was when I was nineteen to twenty-one years old.*

This did not sound at all like the nun who was seated before me.
It was hard to think of her as completely immersed in art. When had
she begun to feel that her vocation might lie somewhere else?

*Then I went to Greece for the first time. I got a scholarship from
Berlin to study there for one month. We were sent in a group of
twenty people to Naxos, to an old Catholic monastery which had
some connections with my art academy. It was very, very beautiful. We could draw, we could take pictures, and we could sculpt,
because there was a sculpture studio. It was very beautiful.*

*I went to Greece, and I didn't even know that Greece was an
Orthodox country. I didn't know what "orthodoxy" was. I went
there for art. I went there with a friend of mine. She was a vio-
linist from England.*

*We were very close together. We always went for walks in the
evenings, and there was a very nice Orthodox monastery just on
top of the rocks opposite the monastery where we were living. It
was a white building, very big, with gigantic stone walls. Saint
Chrysostomos was the name of the monastery. Always we went
up there, but the door was closed. One day we met someone who
let us in. It was very hot outside; it was very, very quiet and cool*

inside. Inside there was shade, very nice, and you just saw the blue sky. There was a nun who welcomed us, and she gave us something to drink and to eat. We went into the church, a very beautiful old church. We liked it very much. We had been going to the cathedral, the main church of the island, every Sunday.

Whenever I traveled to other countries, I always was very interested to see churches and what the people believed in. I think this was part of my searching. I was trying to find out where is God, who is God? And I didn't feel satisfied at all with where I came from, although I had also looked very much in Germany in the Protestant student communities, but I never felt any touch with it. When we were in this monastery this day, Elder Dionysios came suddenly.

Now the story took on new meaning for me. This was the same Elder Dionysios from the symposium of the week before.

He came to the island of Naxos for only one day. It was the feast day of St. John, the author of Revelation. Right beside the monastery there is a small chapel right in the rocks, a cave which is a church named for St. John. The tradition says that when John was at Patmos he passed through Naxos.

This day when we were in this monastery and met Elder Dionysios for the first time, he talked very little. He came to hold confession in Naxos on his way to another island.

As she recalled these events she was animated and spoke with such reverence of the encounter with Elder Dionysios. She didn't speak a word of Greek at that time. She and her friend had been searching for someone who could speak English, and when Elder Dionysios did, they felt it was an answered prayer.

He asked where we came from and for our names and then, abruptly, he asked whether we would make our hearts churches of Christ. We were both very surprised and touched, and we did-

Elder Dionysios

n't know what to answer. My friend didn't say anything, and I said, "I don't know, yes, but maybe it's difficult." And he said, "Yes, it's difficult."

His question touched me so much, just the question and just the idea that you can make your heart really a church of Christ—that Christ lives in your heart and there He is born. With only this one question, I was completely attracted. We had to leave from the monastery but we saw him again in the town, the next day, Sunday. He held liturgy, and we didn't know that he would hold the liturgy but I was just hoping, and I said to my friend, "Let's go. Maybe he is there. Maybe there's a chance to talk with him, because to whom else can we talk here? Nobody speaks English."

We went there when he was just finishing. We learned that he was from Holy Mountain [Mount Athos]. We told him about our interests and about our search and asked him if we could visit a Greek Orthodox monastery. He told us about one in the north of Greece. He said that there was an American novice and also a

German novice, and we could go there and just ask for their names and speak to them, asking them all our questions.

So we stopped our scholarship. We still had two weeks to go, but after one or two days we felt inside that we could not continue our work there as we did before, not at all, because something had happened inside us and we didn't feel quiet. We felt that this time we had still in Greece we wanted to use in another way. We felt that there was something very important we could learn, so we left all the group.

Only a spiritual search of such intensity could interfere in the planned order of their lives. Their fellow students were stunned:

They thought that we were crazy because they knew that it had something to do with the church, but this was a very, very deep impression for both of us. We left them, and we went with a train to north Greece to this monastery. It was a very big monastery with 120 nuns. It was probably the beginning of our knowing that we wanted to become nuns. My friend is a novice now, she didn't become a nun yet. The nuns we met were all very young, all very educated. Many spoke English or foreign languages. There was an immediate contact, a personal connection with the place and all the nuns.

Sister Diodora explained that the regimen of the monastery they visited was strict. The nuns arose at 3 A.M. and had liturgy until 5:30 A.M.

It was the first time for me that I went to church for so much time. There I was in a sanctuary, surrounded with nuns that were singing, chanting. It was so beautiful. The Ormylia Monastery is known in all of Greece for the chanting. When I was there in the church for so long, just standing there listening to the chanting and the prayers, I cried all the time—three hours continuously— I cried so much, and suddenly inside me, so many things happened and I felt I had found what I wanted, the way of life I was looking for during all the years. I understood suddenly why art never really satisfied me deeply. I was busy with it all the day but it didn't satisfy me. I wasn't quiet.

This short series of events—really only two encounters in Greece—changed the whole direction of Diodora's life. What of her training in art? What of her talent? Was it all to be forgotten?

I do art now. I draw. I learned icon painting. I believe that every work for your hands needs an education for your eyes, and this education for the eyes I had in this academy. It's not important that the things I did then were abstract art and now the things I do are different.

The education I received to work with my eyes and my senses helps me very much for everything I do now. For every work in the church I do, for every icon I put on the wall, for everything I restore, for everything I sew, for every work in the garden I do—everywhere, really, whatever you do, you paint.

She spoke with such energy. She drew me into her world of shape and color. I love to "paint" in my photographs—to measure the light, the shadow, the depth of color, and to let the camera be my brush. It is a frame of mind, an attitude, to see the world in this way, through the eyes of an artist. Diodora and I recognized together that God himself is the greatest Artist of all. The world is his palette!

When I lived in Greece I learned also to do mosaics, and I learned to make a model of very difficult Byzantine decorations and Byzantine lettering—engraving—you have plates of marble and you carve it out. I learned this art, and I love it very much. Whenever I have the opportunity, I like to do it. But it's not that I need to do it every day. The other things I am doing are different.

I do it with a very different conscience now than I had before. This is the difference. Before, I did it for myself. Like most of the people who are busy with art like I was, they do it for themselves and they believe they are the creators. I do it now to serve and to glorify God, not to put myself in front and say that I'm the creator of this and I'm an artist but to underline and to show the Creator. This is the difference, I think.

She hadn't jettisoned all her love of art or the training that had prepared her to use her talent. She hadn't sacrificed all of that to become a nun. Rather, she had brought it all along—the invisible gift. It was still a gift she was giving but in a new way.

We spoke then of teaching. We agreed that to be a teacher is to be a window. Sister Diodora responded enthusiastically, "This is what I believe the meaning of a teacher is. Not to put yourself in front, but to put your pupils in front of the reality."

How wise. The contemplative life, which allows one time to ponder and consider ideas, must contribute to such wisdom. Living in Jerusalem had also had a profound effect on her thinking.

I went back [to Berlin] because I hadn't finished my art studies yet. I went back to make an exhibition, which was the midterm exam, the big midterm exam.

But when I was in Berlin, I was sitting in my studio, and all I could think of were my experiences in Greece. I felt so deeply about them that I could not continue. I felt that I had found something that I wanted to get to know more. So I was sitting in the studio, and instead of working on my things which I had to do, I was thinking of how I could organize my life from now on. I had gotten very good marks, but I just wasn't interested anymore.

I felt very close to one of my professors, so I just told him how I felt, that I wanted to stop, because I didn't see any meaning in it anymore. He told me to take a year off, which I had the right to do as a student there. "Then after this year," he said, "you can get out of the school, or see if things change and you choose to continue." I said okay and agreed to do what he said, but I was one hundred percent sure that I knew what my decision would be.

After one year, I wrote him a letter from Greece, and I said to him, "Remember when you advised me a year ago?" We have a saying in German, "If you fill a bowl with soup, you have to finish the soup." So I said to him, "Now you must help because I want to live in Greece. I've started to study theology, but I am still thinking to finish my studies in Berlin. Would you please help me and give me permission to do my artwork in Greece and to send you pictures of my work so you can criticize me in letters and reviews?"

He was so kind to do this, which is very special. He did not have to do it. His name was David Evison. He was English. He wrote very kind critiques and letters. He helped me to continue my studies but to work in a studio in Naxos. Every now and then when I had time I worked on my art, by correspondence, but mostly I was studying theology at the same time in Athens and learning Greek.

In all of this, Elder Dionysios, by his guidance, advice, and help, was teaching me everything and becoming my spiritual father. He is really the beginning, and now, the bridge, which brings me to where I am now and is still being the bridge for me to receive Christ in every moment, in everything.

Again I was aware of the profound influence Elder Dionysios had on Sister Diodora, who at the time of which she was speaking was still Charlotte Stapenhorst, student and willing investigator, soon-to-be convert to Greek Orthodoxy.

Sister Diodora's descriptions of her baptism in the River Jordan and the ritual of becoming a nun allow us an intimate glimpse of the processes that led her out of the mainstream of worldly pursuits and into her personal pilgrimage of peace, tracing the steps of Christ.

My godfather gave me this journey as a present—a pilgrimage to Jerusalem to be baptized in the Jordan River together with my friend who was with me in Naxos. This was Easter time 1988.

We went to the Jordan River, and we went into the water with bathing suits. We were completely immersed three times.

The priest asks us if we repel the devil, and we answer three times, yes. Then he asks us three times if we will follow Christ, and we answer, yes, we will follow Him. Then we have to spit on the ground, and we have to make prostration. Then he asks us if we repulse him, [the Devil], and we say, yes, we repulse him, three times again. Then he asks, "Do you surely follow Christ?" and we say, "Yes, we do." This is the first part; then we come to the water again.

Before we go into the water, we are completely covered with oil by the godmother. On all the body they put the oil. Then we go into the water, and we go three times down. In the case of a small child, the priests put the child three times completely underneath, and say, "In the name of the Father, of the Son, and of the Holy Spirit." But I just went in myself.

Then you come out, and you're dressed in all white clothes. Long white clothes and also a veil. Baptism is always the same.

The priest takes a holy unction, which is especially blessed. Then he blesses you on the head, on the mouth, on the eyes, on the ears, that you'll hear Christ and he also says you're blessed, and you'll serve Christ, that you'll follow Christ. He blesses you on your legs, and on your hands, and on your knees, and on your feet, and on your neck.

Then also he takes the scissors, and he cuts in the form of the cross a little bit of your hair. Then a cross is given to you, and then this ceremony is a part of you. You say the creed of what you believe. I believe in one God, Father Almighty. You say the Nicene Creed.

So the baptism is the door, the beginning, the start of a new life for you because it always goes along with one's confession from childhood until the present. The tears during the confession [repentance] and the waters of the baptism wash you clean in the Holy Spirit and you become a new person in Christ.

She had come to this sacred experience with a group of pilgrims who came from Greece and were visiting the different tourist places. Back in Greece, she studied the Greek language and applied to the theological school. But she had already decided not only to become Greek Orthodox but also to become a nun.

I said very soon to my spiritual father that I wanted to become a nun. But I had the possibility to study at the university, and I was enjoying very much reading of many things I had felt before. It had already filled me very much inside. But I had the thirst to read and to learn more, to learn all about the history and development, and everything.

It was wonderful to read these theological studies there at the University of Athens. For me it was not at all like studies, but just food for my soul.

We studied the New Testament, the Old Testament, the prophets. We read interpretations, and we have translations. We learned lots of Hebrew. We learned Greek. We learned dogma. We learned church history, the different periods. Also we have classes in philosophy.

How well I understood these feelings. I too love to learn and feel my soul being fed. I love to study the Old Testament and the New Testament. It's perfect joy for me. It makes me happy. Sister Diodora agreed quickly, saying, "It's a constant coming up, a step forward on your way to progress."

Sister Diodora graduated from the University of Athens in June 1992. "Then in January 1993, I had to go to Germany to make my final big exhibition in Berlin."

This combining of her disparate interests was amazing to me. How wise of those who supervised her spiritual development to allow her the time to complete her art studies in very nearly the time frame she had planned! She seemed so settled as a nun that I could hardly believe that only a few months before she had been in Berlin with her final big art exhibition. I asked her when exactly she had taken her vows to become a nun.

> *Last year, last summer it happened through the offices of the Jerusalem Patriarch. He came to Greece in June 1992. I became a nun just before my last exam at the University. My last exam I had as a nun. It was an oral exam, and the theology teacher had seen me three days before in lay clothing. I hadn't said anything to him. He was crying when he saw me because he was so touched. He gave me many blessings and good wishes.*

My curiosity about the process of becoming a nun led me to ask her how it was done. She explained that during the time she was a novice, she wore simple clothing but no uniform. Because she was a student and a novice, she did not dress differently from the other students except that she always wore skirts, never trousers. She seemed eager to share each detail. As she spoke, it was as if it were happening all over again:

> *There's no rule for how long one remains a novice. We don't say that you have to be two, three, four, five years a novice, because always it depends on the individual and on the spiritual Father who knows you and who guides you. He decides. I was a novice for five years because of my finishing my schooling, although I was ready from the first moment. But I waited. God made the things in such a way that it happened last year. It was my turn. Very suddenly.*

Her turn came suddenly because the Patriarch of Jerusalem went to Greece, where Sister Diodora was with Elder Dionysios and the rest of his spiritual children. The Patriarch had known Elder Dionysios for a long time and asked him to go with his spiritual children to the Holy Land and establish a women's and a men's monastery there. The Holy Cross Monastery would be used for the men, and for the women, it was his choice. There were many opportunities and possibilities. Sister Diodora described with such tenderness the invitation to come to the holy city of Jerusalem.

So when the Jerusalem Patriarch came to Greece, it was for us like a present. We took his blessing, and Father Dionysios said, "These are my children. These are my sheep, and we will come; she, and she, and she." Then we were four girls who were ready to become nuns and had wanted to for a long time. When I took his blessing, the father said, "She's ready. She's finished all her studies." Then the Patriarch said, "I don't see why we don't make her a nun." So it came very quickly and very surprisingly, and it was a very big joy for all of us because it came so unexpectedly at this moment.

Right away we went to the church and the celebration was held, which is combined with many different chants and prayers. There was again the cutting of the hair in the form of the cross. An abbess who came from a monastery in Greece, she gave to us the dresses. We dressed in them. We put on the veils.

We took the blessing of the Patriarch, and he gave us a cross and read a prayer over us. From that moment we were dressed in black. Black is a symbol for death, because we die, not only in the baptism we die and are reborn in Christ, but also through the tonsure we die completely for the outside life and we follow Christ. It is from that event when we are dressed in black, that we, as the prayers say, take the cross on our shoulders, and we leave our family behind, and we follow him in every step.

We never marry because the event of becoming a nun is like a marriage with Christ. It is a commitment we have. We cannot marry afterwards. We give all, yes, everything, everything. You have given yourself. You don't belong to yourself anymore.

She told me this with total enthusiasm. Everything I observed in her as we became friends testified to her complete commitment to this giving of herself totally to Christ. She had had to switch her family loyalties to a spiritual father, Elder Dionysios, who seemed to have complete responsibility for her destiny. Indeed, her life was no longer her own. She explained that every women's monastery has such a spiritual Father and confessor who takes confessions and administers the sacraments. Even her name was chosen by the Elder Dionysios, after Diodoros, the Patriarch by whom she was tonsured.

This switch of loyalties from family to church is apparent in her daily life. Her parents can visit her at the monastery and she can go to visit them, but even her brother's wedding did not draw her away.

> *My mother and father, they suffer very much because they raised me and knew me as their child, and it's difficult.*
>
> *My mother came to visit me in Greece. When I told her I wanted to become a nun, she said, "It's so strange because I know I have five other children. But at this moment you are my only child. This is how I feel now. This is why I'm crying, and I feel pain so much." I understand that probably it will be impossible for them to completely understand because it is a vocation and it's something that spoke in my heart.*
>
> *I cannot understand and explain how it came, because before I never, never would have thought to go into a monastery and become a nun. It came so suddenly for them. They would prefer to see me as a married woman with children and their grandchildren.*

All at once I was able to identify with the parents of this promising young artist. They respected her quest, realizing she had been searching for spiritual fulfillment and felt she had now found it. Yet, they felt she had somehow stopped being a person, had left the usual path of wife and mother for a way that led away from family forever.

> *They see that I subject myself, and they feel that I stop being a personality. I see exactly opposite. I become a personality just now, before I was not. I did not exist. I was looking and I was doing different things, but I did not have my personality, which God gave me, and which only through Christ I can find. So I found myself instead of losing myself.*

Her eyes were all alight as she described the scene of her "marriage with Christ." I could not have described my own wedding day with more excitement, even the light in the eyes. The wedding day is one of the most memorable of women's transitions as we move from being separate to the risk and hope of unity, oneness.

I remembered the simple details of my own marriage ceremony, the soft touch of the veil around my face. I asked Sister Diodora about the black veil she wore that covered only her forehead and swept down over her head past her ears and under her chin, framing her lovely features in great simplicity and beauty.

> *It is mainly for hiding yourself. It is because we stop being a woman. Our hope and light are the angels. We have to become the angels of the world, for the people in the world. So this is why we cover everything, because we stop being a body. We should not be a personality with a hairstyle, and this, and this, and this. We should be just like an angel, serving and glorifying and serving the people and serving Christ and God.*
>
> *We think of Christ growing inside us, not being something else anymore. Just Christ. This is our way in the monastery, and this is the way our life goes, towards Christ. Christ grows more and more in us, so that we become more one with him. When we read the Bible it becomes more our own story and part of us.*

We spoke again of Diodora's spiritual father, the Archimandrite Dionysios. She seemed content to be in his "family." I asked her how many spiritual children he had.

> *Many, many. I don't know. Hundreds. In Greece he has many and also in other countries. And here in Jerusalem in the Holy Cross Monastery he has twelve men now. Not all are priests; some are monks. I think two or three are now novices.*

As she explained her belief to me, it was easy to see how integrated these ideas were in her present life. It was as if she leaned into the wind of the Spirit and it not only supported her body but carried her gently along the saintly path she had chosen.

I remember well a day I joined her in her work, which included the refurbishing of the chapel in the Patriarch's compound on the Mount of Olives. She had been anxious about finishing the cleaning and polishing of the chapel by a deadline, which was fast approaching. The Patriarch would be coming to entertain some dignitaries there. So I offered to help Sister Diodora and Eleni finish the task. She was surprised when I said how much I loved to polish brass. She set me to polishing the brass box for offerings and another lovely, ancient brass piece.

I could hear her singing as she moved to another area to continue her work there. She did everything from touching up painted frescoes to sweeping the dusty floors and washing the windows, which surely had been stained with hundreds of years of grime. Sister Diodora stepped up to each task and hummed or sang as she worked. She wore a black apron over her black habit and it was dusty and dirty. She worked with great vitality.

These were not the only kinds of things she did. At the Monastery of the Holy Cross, she had spent days, maybe weeks, cleaning the ancient frescoes in the large chapel. I saw the work progress in stages, as the brightened paintings shone even in the dark chamber. She also applied her talents in the painting of icons. Though we had planned to look at icons she had painted, I never had that chance. She did show me her art portfolio, however, so I saw samples of her work.

She used her talents in the redecoration of the Monastery of The Holy Cross. The room for receiving guests had been recently furnished with tastefully upholstered couches and chairs. Whenever I saw vases of fresh flowers there, I wondered if these were not the work of Sister Diodora.

Some of my favorite memories are of our walks on the Mount of Olives. I also treasure our times working together, either at her beautiful walled compound, where we swept chapel floors and polished brass that had long been neglected, or in the Jerusalem Center or in my home.

How could I have foreseen that my final days of packing to leave Jerusalem would be lightened in every way by Sister Diodora? She was on hand to help me pack the books and files and objets d'art in my office, and later, my precious treasures at my home, as my husband and I prepared to return to the United States. She was the personification of her words, "Whenever something comes up, we have to give everything."

As I prepared to leave Jerusalem, a city I had loved for many years, she quietly gave me her everything; her encouragement, her support, even the tedious packing of my belongings with such loving care. It felt good to be in touch with Sister Diodora in this unexpected way. Even though our paths would lead us away from each other, our common caring kept us close.

She often called in the morning to see how my spirits were. Was I especially sad as I prepared to leave after nearly five years in this golden city? Did I need some more physical help moving out of my office—which she knew I loved dearly with its bubbling fountain just outside the window? How many times had we sat together there, silently savoring the sunlit green vines climbing the white walls and the birds, splashing in the fountain?

The moment I mentioned I was packing my office books and files, she came right over. Her ancient little red car appeared, and there she was at my side, soothing away any anticipated loneliness by her sheer joy. We had memorable conversations as we placed my treasures in stark cardboard boxes supplied by the shipping company. I would explain why I kept the photo of students by the ancient olive tree. She would delight in my delight. I pointed out each child and grandchild in the family photo I was reluctant to consign to any box. She would help me decide whether this item or that was important enough to pack in my hand-carried luggage. I was prone to carry everything close to my heart—which was, of course, impossible. She quietly assured me that the things in the boxes would likely arrive safely. Sometimes she said she would pray for that. And I would quiet myself and continue the painful process of preparing to depart.

I would say that it felt like one of my own daughters was helping, but that would not explain it fully. My daughters looked out at me from that prized photo, and Sister Diodora was here and now. She was like my own, but in addition she was a constant friend, singing to me the song in my heart when I was finding it difficult to remember the tune.

As I put a few things aside to give away, she told me how happy she was on the day she gave away everything she owned to become a nun. The contrast in attitude was stunning. I was sobered because I had felt so virtuous in preparing to give a few castoffs to the poor.

She labeled everything carefully. Perhaps I should have suspected something when I saw her writing on sticky labels at such length. She often said how she wished she might be with me to help me unpack, because that would be a real task. Only upon unpacking did I realize what she had been doing beyond the simple labeling of files and photos. She was with me as I unpacked. Small notes in her unmistakable, artistic handwriting were tucked here and there, pressed onto carefully wrapped precious things in smaller boxes inside the larger crates. They were often written in Greek expressions simple enough that she knew I could decipher them. I remember especially "Agape en Christos," which means roughly "Love in Christ." It was as if she had come home with me to help me unpack. Her joy was tangibly there as I opened each object that she had carefully packed so that it could make it all the way home.

We met again a year later when my husband and I traveled to Jerusalem with two teenage granddaughters and were guests at the Monastery of the Holy Cross where she ministered to all of us under the direction of the formidable Elder Dionysios. I was so happy to introduce her to my granddaughters. The girls loved her immediately, just as I had at our first meeting.

Sometimes now we speak on the phone at Christmastime, and it is one of my favorite gifts to hear her gentle voice again. She often says in her letters, "You are with me always." It is easy to feel the same about her. She is such a cherished part of my days. Each thought of her brings a smile and a memory. I remember her packing my bright yellow shoulder bag. She tried it on over her black habit and took a little skip. "It suits you," I told her. "Keep it!" We both doubled up with laughter as I asked her to repeat the performance so I could take a photo.

I wrote to Sister Diodora some time later when she was having an extended visit to Greece. My dear friend Ulwiya Husseini was gravely ill with cancer and had gone to Athens to stay with her daughter for a few weeks. I had had only a moment's visit with her and was worried about her emaciated body but more about her despondent mood. I thought instantly of Sister Diodora and wrote her, asking that she call on Ulwiya and try to cheer her. My message said in part:

> *Elder Dionysios said that he gives his blessing for you to visit my good friend, Ulwiya Husseini. She is in treatment for cancer and after her chemotherapy here she spends the three weeks there just outside of Athens with her daughter. I spent yesterday afternoon with her and met her daughter. Since I cannot visit her again because she flew to Athens today, I knew that you could carry on my mission of love.*
>
> *You could call her and tell her you are my friend and that I have asked you to visit her. Maybe you should mention that you are a nun or you could carry a yellow bag. (Remember?)*
>
> *We will feel connected and close as you do this. You are never far away from me.*

Sister Diodora's response a month later included the following:

> *I was very glad to be able to get to know Mrs. Ulwiya Husseini and I thank you for your idea. Mrs. Ulwiya is a very kind lady. We had an interesting conversation. She has suffered much pain in the last years in her family and seemed tired [her husband and son and mother had died within three years of each other]. Of course, also the chemotherapy is very exhausting. I know it from my own mother.*
>
> > *Always remembering you and your warm smile.*
> > *[signed] Sister Diodora Monache [Nun]*

Abbess Diodora

After the visit with our granddaughters, she wrote me a lovely letter that ended with the words: "Many warm regards to your children and grandchildren. You must send us at least two each year, so that we get to know them all one day!" She knew that would be a long process since we have sixteen grandchildren. But the invitation was absolutely sincere. I would like nothing better than to have all my children and grandchildren accept her loving invitation!

Since our interview, Diodora has been elevated to the office of abbess. She is responsible for a new and growing monastery for women and now lives north of Athens. Her peacefulness is tangible.

The serenity that surrounded her in Jerusalem has surely trailed behind her like her billowing robes as she teaches by her life the art of being an instrument of God's peace.

14. Therefore, What?

HOW VIVIDLY I SEE THESE TWELVE WOMEN WHO HAVE lived and worked in Jerusalem. Each one is amazing. The common denominator they all share is their ability to bring peace to their chaotic surroundings. As you ponder their lives, I hope you will ask, "Therefore, what? What does this all mean to me?"

In choosing individuals to represent the women of Jerusalem, I cut straight across the lines that normally divide the peoples of this complicated region. It was clear from the outset that no one woman could possibly represent the diversity of today's sprawling city.

Some were my friends before I interviewed them. All are my friends now. These friendships, old and new, have enriched me in tangible ways. I see in these twelve women eloquent answers to the day-to-day concerns of women everywhere in our world.

I was surprised to find connections between them. How well I remember speaking with Hind Husseini, a Muslim, about her happiest childhood memory and discovering that it was a Christmas spent with Bertha Spafford Vester, a Christian and the first woman I met in Jerusalem. I never dreamed that many of these women would have been in and out of each other's lives, like lively butterflies.

I have tried to paint true pictures, but they are tiny cameos rather than larger-than-life murals. The daily deeds of these women speak for themselves and are writ large, though they are sometimes only hinted at in these pages. The story of each one's life could fill a book.

They are remarkable women. They are determined women. They love wholeheartedly. Each has a vision, a hope of what can be. This is their strength. They are not to be denied.

Their various faiths anchor them. I learned that for most of them God is real. For some He can almost be touched. Their faith adds a necessary dimension to their lives in good times and in bad.

As I spoke to these women I kept hearing the biblical words of Proverbs 31:10: "Who can find a virtuous woman? for her price is far above rubies." I had found these virtuous women almost without looking for them. Surely the person who penned those lines and the stunning description that follows had known at least one remarkable woman of Jerusalem in antiquity—and may have found, even as I have, that virtue can be contagious and transcends time.

In addition to the goodness extolled in Proverbs, I am keenly aware that these modern women have weaknesses. However, the beauty of their daily deeds, their service to others, somehow supersedes those imperfections. Had I lived with them day to day, I might have become more aware of the negatives in their lives. Instead, my time with them was spent in exploring their dreams, aspirations, motives, hopes, and fears. I came away full of respect and love. Perhaps there is a lesson here. When we pause, willing to search for good in real life, are we not each other's consummate tutors? True peace may finally be found only as we find a way to plumb the depths of each other's hearts.

A quality of softness can be found in the Middle East, unobserved today in the wake of wars. It is part of an ethic of warm hospitality that permeates the predominantly Arab and Israeli culture. It predates all of us by thousands of years. We read about it in the story of Abraham and Sarah's care of those who wandered into their desert home. Likewise, I found a gentle welcome in the home of each of these twelve women. They always found the time to sit a while, sipping something cool and refreshing, so that returning to the desert would be less oppressive.

The lives of these women centered on others in the human family as well as their own kin. Perhaps mothering doesn't happen only when one biologically gives birth. Perhaps *mother* is just another name for peacemaker. Might this selflessness emerge in every situation if we let it? Could the qualities of empathy and compassion be nurtured? I have *seen* peacemaking and *felt* it as I reached to understand the reaching of these twelve women.

The first three women whose stories I have told are now dead, but thankfully, I knew them alive. I have watched as death has touched some of the others. Their responses have taught me how one can meet such inevitabilities and still find peace even in the hour of death and separation.

How lovingly and tirelessly Betty Majaj, the administrator and nurse, looked after her declining but still smiling doctor-husband, Amin. Joyfully they celebrated their fiftieth wedding anniversary as his heart slowly failed. Months later I watched their tender parting at his death. Suddenly she was uncoupled, after more than fifty years with this sweet, brilliant, beloved man. I could not doubt her grief, nor could I miss her dogged determination to go on doing all the good in her power—though now, to do it alone.

Mary Franji, another trained nurse, had been widowed and alone for many years. She sat at the bedside of Anna Grace Lind, her lifelong friend, in Anna Grace's final days. It was nearly a month of sitting. Mary spoke of those days as precious. It never entered her mind that there could be anything she had to do nearly as important as that simple act of helping her friend, to ease her dying. She spoke of the moment of her friend's passing with tenderness and love. Mary did not fear death for her friend or for herself. There is a faith here that can turn away fear, "Perfect love casts out all fear" (1 John 4:18). Had her vigil not been something very close to perfect love?

Vera Ronnen worked tirelessly to save her daughter, Keren, from the cancer that was siphoning away her life. Vera rushed to her daughter's side and helped deal with doctors, hospitals, and a worldwide search for matching stem cells, which was carried on vigorously. But in the end Keren slipped away. As she struggled to live with that awful loss, Vera continued to create. It was her therapy, her way to learn to live again.

Ulwiya Husseini's life was crowded with deaths during the first years of our friendship. First her adored husband, and then her mother and adult son were snatched from her. What had been a congenial and orderly life went into a tailspin. What a tutorial it was to watch her falter, grieve deeply, and finally fight her way back, even past her own threatened death from cancer, to live one day at a time, not just resigned but with joy. When she began to garden again and to give away the flowers, I knew she was healing. Lines from the prophet Micah come to mind. "Rejoice not against me, O mine enemy: when I fall, I shall arise; when I sit in darkness, the Lord shall be a light unto me" (Micah 7:8). We fall many times, but all is not lost providing we arise just once more.

These responses to adversity and suffering represent a hard-won attitude. Experience, regardless of its severity, usually results in a measure of earned maturity. Patience and personal peace can be the prize.

When I telephoned Sahir Dajani on a recent trip to Jerusalem to arrange a visit, her happy voice greeted me. We exchanged news of both our families in detail as we began planning to meet. Suddenly she remembered that she was having surgery on both her feet in a couple of days. When I called to see how her surgery had gone, I heard the same happy voice, though she was confined to bed for three weeks. I was struck with the way she simply accepted what had to be done—and her attitude even included joy. Someone once taught me that pain is inevitable but misery is optional.

A few years ago at a university commencement I heard Jehan Sadat, widow of Anwar Sadat, address the graduates. The recipient of an honorary degree, she had come to speak of peace. How ironic that Anwar Sadat made his momentous trip from Egypt to Jerusalem to find peace for his people. That journey started a chain reaction that eventually proved fatal for him. Peace exacts a high price.

Mrs. Sadat spoke of the bridges of peace that are built with kindness and understanding. She suggested that the university of peace is the home, and mothers are the first professors, with their gentle spirits and unselfish love, their wanting for others what they want for themselves. She indicated that the path to peace is found through our hearts and that we must each search our own heart to find that path. Ordinary people, she said, can change the world by reaching beyond themselves when their situation demands it. She cited the examples of Gandhi, Nelson Mandela, Mother Teresa and her own husband, Anwar Sadat.

My examples are these twelve women of Jerusalem. Observing their lives, I have developed new compassion for the women suffering on both sides of a devastating, ongoing conflict. I feel empathy for both. It is a 100 percent feeling that shifts from one side to the other as tragedy piles on tragedy.

How can I possibly take sides? I'm neither Palestinian nor Israeli. I look at both sides and see values that have become skewed. Retaliation as a national policy is a value shared by each side in the conflict. What a roadblock to peace! I see good things, too, such as continuing friendships between Arabs and Jews in neighborhoods. These bonds have been pushed underground by threatening circumstances.

It's hard to live in the middle of conflict and not want to fix it. Perhaps that's why I'm so mesmerized by news from the Middle East. I am always curious to see what other people are doing when they are in a position to make a difference, hopeful that something can start the healing. Something in all of us longs for peace for these beleaguered people. There must be another road, one not traveled, not yet found.

The truth is we are each a maker of peace. "Peace cannot be imposed," taught church leader Ezra Taft Benson. "It must come from the lives and hearts of men [and women]. There is no other way."[1]

Peace is a vital part of life at home or in the workplace. One can learn to capture peace; by some miracle to dissuade others from discord. A wife makes peace with her husband, seeking it everywhere and by any means she can. A mother continually negotiates for peace among her teasing children. A teacher must build an atmosphere of peace if she is to teach anything to anyone. Nothing really works without peace.

These twelve women of Jerusalem teach with their lives that such peace is possible. They cling to hope. It sustains them from day to day. Emily Dickinson points us towards this tenacious attitude in her poem "Hope":

Hope is the thing with feathers—
That perches in the soul—
And sings the tune without the words—
And never stops—at all—
And sweetest—in the Gale—is heard—
And sore must be the storm—
That could abash the little Bird—
That kept so many warm—
I've heard it in the chillest land—
And on the strangest Sea—
Yet, never, in Extremity,
It asked a crumb—of Me.

These women have maintained their vision of peace through unwavering hope. They show us that nothing is impossible by daily doing the impossible. Their faith and sense of meaning continue to be the energy that fuels their lives. Their agenda is whatever needs doing. Credit for success is usually deflected to others. They feel no need to count the cost or keep receipts for reimbursement. Though blame may surface after each act of violence inflicted on their community, it has no permanent place in their hearts. That would be a waste of valuable time and energy. They take responsibility for whatever they can do and leave others to do the same. And when they are down and everything looks the darkest, they get up one more time.

Saint Francis of Assisi wrote the prayer for peace that describes the twelve women you have met in these pages:

Lord, make me an instrument of thy peace.
Where there is hatred, let me sow love . . .
Where there is despair, hope,
Where there is darkness, light,
Where there is sadness, joy.
Lord, make me an instrument of thy peace.

As I began this project, my goal was to explore how the women of Jerusalem felt in their hearts about the possibilities for peace. Did they harbor hope for an outcome that would mean peaceful coexistence? Did they feel powerless in the face of so much conflict and violence boiling around them? These were my questions. But the very act of asking them changed my focus to their agendas. After all, the question of peace is a matter of life and death in their city.

I was stunned to find that not one of them felt powerless. Living on the edge had honed them, strengthened them in ways they might never have imagined possible. There were chasms to be crossed, but they had learned to be their own bridges. They somehow found the path to peace that leads through their own hearts and the hearts of others. In this beleaguered city, whether at war or fighting for peace, they weren't waiting to see what would happen next. Each, in her own way, was working on the tiny interim miracles she could manage. If the big miracle of political peace materialized, fine, but if it was perpetually postponed, surely more tiny miracles would surface in each of their lives and spread into wider and wider circles. And so it is with us.

Notes

1. Thomas S. Monson, *Peace* (Salt Lake City, Utah: Deseret Book, 1986), 48.

GRATITUDE

Near the place where I pray I keep a Gratitude Journal. In that location, it fills up quite naturally. Using that form, I express my gratitude to those who assisted me with this book. How grateful I am—

For a husband and grown children and grandchildren, who regularly humored my passion for this project, ever willing to listen and sometimes suggest.

For research assistants, who listened carefully to the actual voices of these women as they transcribed my tapes. More than once they would stop and speak of inspiration or simply shed a tear. Each believed I could sift through the hundreds of pages they had typed to make a book.

For the deans and department chairs who sent me these bright, able and caring students.

For a myriad of friends who embraced my Jerusalem women, even though they knew them only through my enthusiastic words.

For the Swimming Women, who saw me first thing in the morning five days a week and became a sounding board for my ideas.

For a handful of devoted friends, who were willing to read my words more carefully with pencil at the ready.

For my agent, Rich Barber, who made me believe this book had to be published and gave it to Gene Gollogly at Lantern Books, who agreed.

For McRay Magleby, whose Wave of Peace has adorned my office walls since Jerusalem days and now graces the cover of this book.

For professionals who became friends and applied their skills to the manuscript: Doris Dant, Suzanne Brady and Sarah Gallogly.

For Erin MacLean at Lantern Books, who put it all together to make a book.

Last, but never least, for Allen Bergin, colleague and friend, who said one day, "Why don't you write a book while you're living in Jerusalem?"